vegan
COMFORT COOKING

vegan COMFORT COOKING

75 Plant-Based Recipes to Satisfy Cravings and Warm Your Soul

MELANIE MCDONALD

Creator of A Virtual Vegan

PAGE STREET
PUBLISHING CO.

PAGE STREET
PUBLISHING CO.

First published in 2019 by

Page Street Publishing Co.

27 Congress Street, Suite 105

Salem, MA 01970

www.pagestreetpublishing.com

Distributed by Macmillan, sales in Canada by The Canadian Manda Group.

23   22   21   20   19   1   2   3   4   5

ISBN-13: 978-1-62414-779-1

ISBN-10: 1-62414-779-8

Library of Congress Control Number: 2018962643

Cover and book design by Rosie Stewart for Page Street Publishing Co.

Photography by Melanie McDonald

Printed and bound in the United States

this is for all of you

All of you who make my recipes and feed them to your loved ones, all of you who share my recipes with your friends or on social media, and all of you who have supported me in this crazy adventure. Without you my little blog would never have grown into what it is today and I would not be writing this book. It is a testament to the fact that you should always follow your dreams, because you never know where they will take you.

Contents

THE MUNCHIES 105

SWEET TALK 135

BITS & BOBS 187

introduction

My passion for creating recipes is something I didn't know existed until I started my blog, A Virtual Vegan, four years ago. I love how my recipes and website draw people together through a common interest in cooking, eating amazing food and living a kind and compassionate life.

How did it all begin? I came to the realization one day that how I was living my life was very wrong.

I remember the day it finally dawned on me clearly. I was at a farm show and I was petting the most beautiful, friendly cow through a fence when over the loudspeaker I heard that he was being auctioned off and would be slaughtered after the show.

Like most people, I was so detached from the reality of where meat actually comes from, that how it gets to the shelf in the grocery store had never really crossed my mind before. The reality suddenly hit me and I turned to my husband and told him that I would never eat meat again. I thought I would become vegetarian. Then the day after, I started to research the dairy and egg industries—and the effect animal products have on our health—and fell into a rabbit hole of horror. I had been living in blissful ignorance my entire life and what I learned shocked me to the core.

I became vegan immediately and, as someone who loves her food, soon realized that there was a real shortage of amazing, flavorful recipes that were as good as nonvegan ones. There was no way my greedy self was going to live life eating disappointing food, and having always loved to cook, I knew I could do better myself.

So, I decided to start a blog to share my own creations. I had no idea what I was doing, and some of my first blog posts and photographs will attest to that, but gradually people started coming regardless and they stuck around and multiplied into the millions that visit every year now. You may be one of those readers, and if so, it is you, your support and your love of my recipes that made this cookbook happen. And, wow, I could not be more grateful. I am getting to do something I truly love as my job: I get to make people happy through food every single day, and I help make a compassionate way of living just as damn tasty as an uncompassionate one. I am so incredibly humbled by this whole experience.

What will you find in this cookbook?

Comfort food! Which, in my opinion, is the best type of food and what I always want to eat. We're talking amazingly tasty, stick-to-your-ribs comfort cooking that will leave you and your family feeling totally satisfied.

There are breakfast and brunch recipes, entrées, snacks and appetizers and, of course, plenty of desserts and yummy baked things. All the recipes are vegan by default but they can and will be enjoyed by everyone, vegan or not.

If, like me in the early days, you have tried other vegan recipes and felt a little let down, then you have arrived in the right place. I'm sorry that you may have had to trawl through some not so good or just average recipes to get here, but without them, this book and my blog might not exist. They were, and still are, my motivation for producing the recipes I do.

I stand by a meme I saw recently that said there should be a refund on calories for things that don't taste as good as expected. Nothing is more disappointing, and it won't be happening on my watch.

Eating vegan food does not mean that you have to give up all your favorite things, and it does not mean that you have to sacrifice flavor or results. You just need to find yourself some damn good recipes.

The good news is that your search is over. Those damn good recipes are here between these covers. I have written this book for you to ensure that your good food drought is over. You will be having your cake and eating it from here on in.

My mission from day one has been to make vegan food that is just as good as its nonvegan equivalent. It has to be good as I'm the only vegan in my family. If they eat my vegan food and love it, it makes the cut. If not, then you won't find it on my blog or in this book. I never sacrifice taste to make something vegan. The same can be said for any of my recipes that happen to be oil-free or gluten-free. If it's here, it's because it has earned its spot, got my family's approval and is seriously yum!

It doesn't stop there, though. Once the recipes have made it past my family, they go on to be tested by my team of amazing recipe testers so that I can be confident they can work as well as possible in kitchens other than mine. Every single recipe is the best it can be and has been developed with depth of flavor in mind. Each individual ingredient plays a part and is important in its own way. Because of this, I recommend that you do not make substitutions for any of the ingredients the first time you make the recipes, unless I specifically state alternatives. By all means, once you have tried a recipe as written, tweak it slightly to suit your tastes, but if you omit or significantly change the listed ingredients, you will likely not get the best results.

Wherever I can, I give instructions on how to make my recipes oil-free because I know many people like to cook that way. However, I will only omit the oil or give alternatives if it doesn't take away from the outcome of the recipe.

Alternatives to oil might be aquafaba (chickpea liquid), nut butter or maybe even water for sautéing (it works surprisingly well!). Some recipes just will not work, or won't be anywhere near as good, if no oil is used, so in those no alternatives are given.

Before getting started, I encourage you to read the entire recipe, including the tips, just in case something needs preparing in advance, or there are components that can be premade up to a few days ahead to make your mealtimes or entertaining easier.

I also highly recommend that you use a digital kitchen scale to weigh ingredients, particularly with recipes that involve flour. You can pick one up for under $10 and it will last for years and years. If you really must use cups, then always spoon flour into the cups, then level off the top with a knife without compacting it or shaking it down into the cup. This will make things a little more consistent and more in line with my measurements. Do not scoop the flour up into the cup, as when you do this, you will end up using much more than was intended and things won't turn out as well as they should.

Almost all the ingredients used in my recipes are available at most grocery stores. A handful, though, may be unfamiliar if you are new to vegan cooking (aquafaba, I'm looking at you!) and if so, you will find a note in the recipe concerned explaining more about it.

I want you to have fun in the kitchen, make and eat what you love and enjoy every single bite. I don't want you feeling the pressure to produce perfection at every turn, but I do want my recipes to turn out the best they possibly can for you. By following my instructions and tips, that's what you will get.

This is cozy, homely, comfort cooking that doesn't have to look perfect. All that matters is that the finished recipes taste amazing and you go away feeling totally satisfied with a full tummy and a happy heart.

My dream is that this book will be the one you turn to when you want and need something truly delicious to eat. I want it to be dog-eared and scattered with crumbs and sticky fingerprints and I want you to enjoy cooking from it as much as I enjoyed creating it.

Put quite simply, if you are looking to reduce or totally cut animal products from your diet for health, ethical or environmental reasons, if you love good food and don't want to sacrifice taste, and if you are even half as greedy as I am, then you need this book and its recipes in your life.

Mel

first, we brunch

I love nothing more than a long, lazy breakfast or brunch. Sitting around a table filled with amazing food, pots of hot coffee, freshly squeezed orange juice and laid-back chat is the way I like to start my weekends.

As they say breakfast is the most important meal of the day, we need to make sure it counts. In this first chapter you will find all sorts of tasty delights, ready and waiting to fill your tummy and your soul.

Your mornings will be a whole lot better when they include any of these must-try recipes. We're talking comfort to the max with everything from perfect fluffy pancakes (page 28) to the breakfast casserole (page 31). There is even cake (page 38)! Because this is my cookbook, and if I can squeeze more cake into my day, I will.

Of course, we don't always have the time to linger for hours over breakfast, which is why I have also included plenty of make-ahead, grab-and-go options, too.

Oh, and just because these recipes appear in the brunch chapter does not mean they need to be restricted to mornings only; many make great lunch box stuffers or snacks. And breakfast for dinner, or "brinner" as I like to call it, is always a good thing!

RUSTIC SKILLET POTATO AND GREENS HASH

yield: 3 or 4 servings

2 tbsp (30 ml) olive oil, divided

1 lb (454 g) potatoes, peeled and cut into ⅜" (1-cm) cubes

1 tsp salt

½ tsp freshly ground black pepper

1 tsp smoked paprika or chipotle powder

1 medium onion, chopped

3 cloves garlic, chopped finely

2 bell peppers, seeded and cut into ⅜" (1-cm)-wide slices (use 2 different colors)

1 bunch (about 7 large leaves or 450 g) lacinato kale (a.k.a. dinosaur, Tuscan or black kale), stemmed and chopped into bite-size pieces

About 30 cherry tomatoes, halved (1½ cups [225 g])

to serve

Salsa

Chopped avocado

When we want something savory, filling and comforting for brunch, this hash is one of our favorites. It transforms a few simple, fresh ingredients into a rustic, tasty skillet of super colorful deliciousness. Smoked paprika is my favorite of all the spices. It brings a unique smokiness to dishes and works really well with the crispy potatoes and tender veggies in this recipe. What's even better is that it reheats really well, so you can make a big batch during the weekend and enjoy leftovers for days after. It's one of those brunch recipes that makes a great dinner, too!

In a heavy-bottomed skillet, heat 1 tablespoon (15 ml) of the olive oil over medium heat. Add the potatoes, salt, black pepper and smoked paprika and toss to coat. Cook for around 20 minutes, or until the cubes are golden brown on all sides. Try to keep them in a single layer in the pan and don't move them too frequently. You want a nice golden crust to develop on each side.

Transfer the potatoes to a small bowl and set aside. Add the remaining tablespoon (15 ml) of oil to the pan and sauté the onion over medium heat for 3 to 5 minutes, or until translucent. Add the garlic and bell peppers and continue to cook for another 5 minutes, or until the bell peppers are just tender. Add the kale and cook, stirring frequently, for 3 minutes, or until tender, then return the potatoes to the pan and add the cherry tomato halves. Toss everything together and let the potatoes and tomatoes warm through for a few minutes.

Serve drizzled with salsa and a scattering of chopped avocado.

Reheat leftovers in a skillet over medium heat, or microwave for a couple of minutes.

BLACK FOREST BREAKFAST CREPES

yield: 6 large crepes

crepes

1½ cups + 3 tbsp (210 g) all-purpose flour

¼ tsp salt

¾ tsp baking powder

½ cup (120 ml) aquafaba (see note)

1¾ cups (420 ml) nondairy milk

2 tbsp (30 ml) mild olive, vegetable or sunflower oil, or melted coconut oil, plus more for skillet

cherry sauce

4 cups (620 g) frozen cherries

3 tbsp (24 g) arrowroot powder or cornstarch

5 tbsp (60 g) cane or granulated white sugar

2 tbsp (30 ml) water or fresh orange juice, plus more to thin, if necessary

1 tsp vanilla or almond extract

Pinch of salt

easy chocolate sauce

⅓ cup (27 g) unsweetened cocoa powder (spooned into the cup, not scooped)

Pinch of salt

¼ cup (60 ml) boiling water

3 tbsp (45 ml) pure maple syrup

½ tsp vanilla extract

Vegan whipped cream, yogurt or ice cream, to serve

I can't imagine how anyone could resist a hot crepe straight out of the pan, but please try, so that you can fill a few of them with vegan whipped cream, yogurt or ice cream, my super-yum cherry sauce and a drizzle of bittersweet chocolate sauce. Want perfect crepes? Be sure to let the batter rest, cook them very quickly and don't sub the aquafaba with anything else! (See my note if you are wondering what the heck aquafaba is!) Never made crepes before? No worries—they are really easy. You will be tucking into a hearty, sauce-drizzled pile of them in no time!

To prepare the crepes, in a medium bowl, whisk together the flour, salt and baking powder. In another bowl, combine the aquafaba, nondairy milk and oil. Stir together, and then pour into the flour mixture. Whisk until the batter is well mixed and most of the lumps have gone. A few small lumps are okay. Leave to rest for at least 10 minutes.

While the batter is resting, prepare the cherry sauce. Place the frozen cherries in a saucepan and sprinkle with the arrowroot powder. Stir to combine. It will look lumpy and strange. Add the sugar, water or orange juice, vanilla and salt. Stir as well as you can; then place over medium heat. The cherries will start to defrost after about 5 minutes and you will be able to stir them more easily. Keep stirring every few minutes until the cherries are soft and the sauce is bubbling and thickened, about 10 minutes. Keep cooking until you get the texture you prefer. The longer you leave the sauce, the jammier it will get. If it gets too thick, add a drop of water and stir to thin it out. Once done, remove from the heat and set aside, uncovered.

In a small bowl, mix together the cocoa powder and salt; then add the boiling water and stir. It will become a really thick paste. Add the maple syrup and vanilla—stir it all really well and it will thin out. Set it aside while you make the crepes. The chocolate sauce will thicken as it sits but can be thinned with a drop more of water, if necessary, just before serving.

Place a nonstick skillet over medium-high heat. Any size skillet is okay; the finished crepes will be the diameter of the skillet you use. Add some oil and wipe it around the pan with a paper towel to coat the whole surface, being careful not to burn your fingers.

(continued)

Once the pan is really hot, you are ready to make the first crepe. Pour the batter into the middle of the pan. I like to use a ladle to do this. In a 10-inch (25.5-cm) pan, you will need about ½ cup (120 ml) of batter per crepe. Immediately pick up the pan and swirl the batter around so it runs around and coats the surface of the pan thinly. You need to do this quickly. Put the pan back on the heat and leave the crepe to cook for between 30 seconds and a minute. Turn back a little of an outside edge to look under and flip or turn the crepe when it is golden in places and some brown spots have appeared. Cook for about another 30 seconds on the other side, or until golden and spotty, too. Then remove from the pan.

Repeat until all of the batter is used, adding another drop of oil and wiping it around the pan before cooking each crepe. You can feed the crepes to the waiting hoards as you cook them, or you can set a plate in a very low oven (about 225°F [110°C]) and place each finished crepe there so they keep warm until you are all done.

Serve the crepes filled with some vegan cream or yogurt, some cherry sauce and a drizzle of chocolate sauce. For dessert, some vegan ice cream is nice, too!

Unused crepe batter will keep in the fridge for a few days. It might thicken up a little, and if it does, just whisk in a little more nondairy milk to thin it out. Cooked crepes can also be kept in the fridge for a few days and reheated quickly in a skillet over medium heat.

Leftover cherry and chocolate sauce will keep in the fridge for up to 1 week. Cherry sauce can be reheated in a pan on the stovetop or in the microwave.

tip: *The crepes are great with all sorts of sweet and savory fillings, so have fun and get creative!*

note: *Aquafaba might sound fancy but it is, quite simply, the liquid hiding in your can of chickpeas. It has a very similar consistency to raw egg white and works incredibly well as an egg replacer. It can also be used when baking such things as homemade fries or roast potatoes, instead of using oil. If you have to open a can of chickpeas just for the aquafaba, once you have drained off the liquid, you can freeze the chickpeas in an airtight container or freezer bag until you need them. If you end up with leftover aquafaba, it freezes very well, too. I tend to use a silicone ice cube mold to freeze it in, so that I have small amounts on hand at all times.*

If you cook your own dried chickpeas, you can make your own aquafaba. Boil the chickpeas as usual until just tender, and then leave them to cool in the water they were cooked in. Then, refrigerate overnight. The liquid will become thick and starchy. Drain them, catching the precious aquafaba, and rinse the chickpeas in a sieve. They are ready to use. If the homemade aquafaba is egg white-y in texture, it is fine to use right away. Sometimes it is still a little thin. If so, reduce it in a pan over medium heat until it has thickened up. Remove from the heat and let cool; then use or store until needed.

OOEY-GOOEY CINNAMON ROLLS

yield: 8 large rolls

rolls

¼ cup (55 g) vegan butter, plus 1 tbsp (15 g) for baking dish

4 cups (500 g) all-purpose flour, plus more for rolling

1 slightly heaping tbsp (10 g) instant or fast-acting yeast

1½ tsp (8 g) salt

⅓ cup (67 g) cane or granulated white sugar

¾ cup (180 ml) unsweetened nondairy milk

¼ cup (60 ml) aquafaba (see note on page 18), for the softest, fluffiest results, or use more nondairy milk

1 tsp vanilla extract

filling

⅓ cup (67 g) soft room-temperature vegan butter

1 cup (220 g) dark brown or coconut sugar

2 tbsp (15 g) ground cinnamon

Pinch of salt

Oh my goodness. I go weak at the knees at the mere thought of these cinnamon rolls drowned in their ridiculously delicious "cream cheese" frosting. They are soft, fluffy, crusty in all the right places, super sticky and ooey-gooey. They will bring on those warm and fuzzy feelings that only home baking can, and turn your kitchen into a place where everyone wants to hang out. If you have a fear of baking with yeast, you must conquer it so that you can satisfy your sticky bun cravings. Stat.

First, prepare the dough. Melt ¼ cup (55 g) of vegan butter gently and set aside to cool. In the bowl of a stand mixer, stir together the flour, yeast, salt and sugar. In a small bowl, mix together the melted butter, nondairy milk, aquafaba and vanilla; then pour into the flour mixture. Attach the dough hook and knead on medium speed for 8 minutes. Alternatively, you can knead the dough by hand for 10 to 15 minutes. The dough should form a nice, smooth, supple, very slightly sticky ball. If it feels dry, add more milk, 1 tablespoon (15 ml) at a time, kneading it in between each addition. If the dough feels too sticky, add a tablespoon (8 g) or two more of flour and knead again to incorporate.

Transfer to a greased bowl, cover with a clean, damp towel or plastic wrap and leave to rest for 15 minutes. While it's resting, use the reserved tablespoon (15 g) of butter to grease an 8-inch (20.5-cm) square baking dish.

Turn the dough onto a lightly floured work surface and roll it out into a roughly 9 x 14–inch (23 x 35.5–cm) rectangle. Stretch out the corners a bit with your hands as you go to help make the dough rectangular.

Prepare the filling. Slather the top of the dough with the softened vegan butter. In a small bowl, mix together the sugar, cinnamon and salt, and sprinkle it evenly over the buttered rectangle, leaving about a 1-inch (2.5-cm) margin around the edges.

Starting from the long edge, roll up the dough into a sausage shape as tightly as you can; then slice it into 8 equal pieces with a very sharp serrated knife. Place each piece, cut side down, in the prepared baking dish. Cover the dish with the damp towel or plastic wrap you used earlier and leave to rise in a draft-free place until doubled. This usually takes 60 to 90 minutes. If you want to speed things up a little, you can put the rolls in the oven with the light on to provide a little warmth.

(continued)

frosting

1 (8-oz [227-g]) package vegan cream cheese

½ cup (110 g) room-temperature vegan butter

1 tsp vanilla extract

1 tbsp (15 ml) pure maple syrup

Pinch of salt

3 cups (360 g) powdered sugar

Once almost doubled, preheat the oven to 350°F (176°C). If the rolls were rising in the oven, be sure to remove them first. Bake for 22 minutes, or a little longer if you want them a bit crustier.

While they are baking, prepare the frosting. In a large bowl or a stand mixer, beat the vegan cream cheese with the vegan butter, vanilla, maple syrup and salt until smooth. Then, gradually add the powdered sugar, about ½ cup (65 g) at a time, beating between each addition, until you have a thick, velvety smooth frosting.

Remove the rolls from the oven and let cool for about 10 minutes; then slather them generously in the frosting. Alternatively, if you are not going to be eating them all right away, let them cool completely and add the frosting just before you serve them.

tips: If you are unable to get vegan cream cheese, frost the cinnamon rolls with 1 cup (130 g) of powdered sugar mixed with 1 to 3 tablespoons (15 to 45 ml) of nondairy milk.

Return leftover cinnamon rolls to their ooey-gooey state by reheating them at 350°F (176°C) for 5 to 6 minutes or by microwaving for 20 to 30 seconds.

Leftover frosting will keep in a sealed container in the fridge for up to 1 week. It's great on cupcakes, pancakes (page 28), French toast (page 23) or used as a dip with fruit or cookies.

THE ULTIMATE FRENCH TOAST

yield: 6 large slices

1 cup (240 ml) nondairy milk

½ heaping, very packed cup (4.6-oz [130-g]) extra-firm tofu (regular, not silken)

2 tsp (10 ml) vanilla extract

2 tbsp (25 g) cane or granulated white sugar

¼ tsp ground cinnamon

⅛ tsp salt

1 tbsp (15 g) vegan butter, plus a little more, or mild oil, for brushing the griddle/pan (optional)

6 (1" [2.5-cm]-thick) slices hearty, crusty vegan white bread (for best results, make sure it is a couple of days old)

This recipe will up your brunch goals in style with its golden, crispy, buttery edges, and perfectly custardy insides. It's great for those times when you feel like eating something elaborate but you're too lazy to give too much effort. Just blend the custard, dip some stale vegan bread slices into it and pan-fry until deeply golden. Tofu might seem like a funny ingredient to add to the custard, but it's what sets this French toast apart from other recipes. Once cooked, the texture is just like that of French toast made with eggs. Accompaniments can be as simple as a generous drizzle of maple syrup or a tumble of fresh berries, but the cherry sauce from my Black Forest Breakfast Crepes (page 17) or the berry sauce from my Dreamy Baked Berry Cheesecake (page 136) are also fantastic with it.

In a blender, combine all the ingredients, except the bread, and blend until completely smooth.

Heat a griddle or skillet over medium heat and brush with a little vegan butter or mild oil. If it's a really good nonstick one, you can get away without greasing it, but the toast won't be quite as golden.

Pour the blended tofu mixture into a wide bowl or a rimmed plate and dip the bread into it. Leave the bread to sit in the mixture for 20 seconds; then turn it over and do the same on the other side. Lift it out and quickly dip all around the edges of the crust, too. Then place each "custardy" slice on the hot griddle. Cook for 4 to 5 minutes on each side, or until very golden— then remove from the griddle and serve immediately.

Leftover "custard" will keep in the fridge for up to 3 days.

BLISSFUL BANANA-PECAN MUFFINS

yield: 8 large muffins

A little vegan butter, coconut oil or any other neutral oil, for pan (optional)

3 medium very ripe and spotty bananas, divided

¼ cup (64 g) soft, drippy room-temperature cashew butter, almond butter, pecan butter or coconut oil

1 tbsp (22 g) blackstrap molasses

1 tsp vanilla extract

½ cup (100 g) cane or granulated white sugar, plus more for sprinkling tops (optional)

½ tsp salt

2 cups (230 g) spelt flour

2 tsp (8 g) baking powder

½ cup (50 g) chopped pecans or walnuts, plus more for sprinkling tops (optional)

You won't find any mini muffins around here. If you are going to indulge in a banana-pecan muffin for breakfast, it needs to be worth your while. We're talking big, hearty and satisfying. Perfect as they are, but even better split and smeared with nut butter!

Preheat the oven to 425°F (218°C) and grease or line 8 wells of a muffin pan.

Chop just three-quarters of one of the bananas into small pieces and set aside. Put the rest of the bananas in a mixing bowl and mash them until they are a puree. I like to do this in my stand mixer fitted with the paddle attachment. It does the job really well, but if you don't have one, you can do this by hand with a fork.

Add the nut butter, blackstrap molasses, vanilla, sugar and salt to the pureed bananas and beat really well. You can do this either by hand or in a stand mixer.

Add the spelt flour and baking powder and stir everything together by hand. It's important not to overmix, so I advise not to use a stand mixer for this part. Stir just enough that you can't see any dry flour.

Add the reserved chopped banana along with the nuts and stir gently to incorporate.

Spoon evenly into the prepared muffin pan. I like to sprinkle a few more nuts and a little sugar onto the top of each muffin for decoration and added texture, but this is optional.

Bake at 425°F (218°C) for 5 minutes; then lower the oven temperature to 375°F (190°C) and bake for a further 15 to 18 minutes. The muffins should be well risen, golden and a toothpick inserted into the middle of a muffin should come out clean.

tips: *To make these muffins nut-free, use sunflower seed butter, pumpkin seed butter or coconut oil instead of the nut butter and replace the nuts with vegan chocolate chips, pumpkin seeds or sunflower seeds.*

You can bake the batter in a 9 x 5–inch (23 x 12.5–cm) loaf pan at 350°F (176°C) for around 50 minutes to make banana bread instead of muffins.

TOFU IN PURGATORY

yield: 2 generous or 4 small servings

1 tbsp (15 ml) olive oil, or 2 tbsp (30 ml) water

4 large cloves garlic, chopped finely

1 (28-oz [793-g]) can diced tomatoes

½ tsp dried red pepper flakes (use less if you prefer less heat, or a little more if you like things spicy)

2 tsp (about 4 g) mixed dried herbs, such as herbes de Provence, Italian seasoning or a combination of thyme, oregano and rosemary

1 tsp cane or granulated white sugar (optional, but helps bring out the tomato flavor)

1 tsp salt, or to taste

½ tsp freshly ground black pepper, or to taste

1 (12- to 14-oz [350- to 400-g]) block medium-firm tofu (no need to press it)

Kala namak (optional; see note)

Crusty vegan bread, for serving

Spice up your morning with this cozy, super-yum, breakfast, brunch or even dinner dish that is made in one pan, from scratch, in about 20 minutes. Traditionally it's made with eggs, but I use medium-firm tofu, which when simmered up in the fiery, garlicky, chunky tomato sauce, becomes silky-soft like egg white in texture. It works so well. Be sure to serve with plenty of crusty vegan bread to mop up every last drop of the spicy sauce!

In a skillet, heat the olive oil or water over medium heat; then cook the garlic for 1 to 2 minutes, or until just starting to turn a little golden.

Add the tomatoes, red pepper flakes, herbs and sugar (if using). Season with salt and pepper to taste—then simmer over medium heat while you prepare the tofu.

Drain the tofu and cut it into 4 evenly sized pieces. First, cut horizontally through the middle to make 2 long pieces, and then cut each of those pieces in half to make 4 squares. If you want to be fancy and have round pieces of tofu like "eggs," use a cookie cutter to cut 4 rounds and save the scraps for another recipe, such as my Go-To Tofu Scramble (page 53).

Gently place the 4 pieces of tofu in the simmering sauce, lower the heat to medium-low and simmer for 15 minutes, or until the sauce is thickening up a little and the tofu is soft and heated through.

Sprinkle each piece of tofu with a little kala namak (if using) just before serving, if you want it to have an "eggy" flavor.

Serve with crusty vegan bread. Leftovers reheat well either in a skillet over low heat or in a microwave.

note: *Kala namak is also known as Indian black salt. It has a really high sulfur content, which makes it smell and taste of egg. It is an amazing ingredient to add to any vegan recipe that emulates an egg dish, such as this Tofu in Purgatory or my tofu scramble (page 53) and in omelets and quiches. Just a tiny pinch is all that is necessary, and a small container of it will last for ages. It isn't yet commonly available in grocery stores, but health food stores, anywhere that specializes in vegan products or online retailers, such as Amazon, stock it. It's well worth seeking out if you miss that "eggy" flavor.*

BEST *EVER* FLUFFY PANCAKES

yield: 8 pancakes

2 cups (250 g) all-purpose flour

2 tbsp (22 g) baking powder

1 tsp salt

2 tbsp (25 g) cane or granulated white sugar

6 tbsp (90 ml) aquafaba (see note on page 18)

2 tsp (10 ml) apple cider vinegar

4 tsp (20 ml) vanilla extract

¼ cup (60 ml) melted vegan butter

1½ cups (360 ml) nondairy milk

Neutral oil or vegan butter, for griddle

If anything is going to compel you to crawl out of your nice warm bed in the morning, it's a stack of fluffy pancakes slathered with vegan butter and maple syrup. This recipe creates pancakes just as good as any I had in my prevegan days. They are incredibly soft and puffy and buttery and dreamy. Perfect for a long, lazy brunch on the weekend! My trick for making them super soft? It's aquafaba! Adding canned chickpea liquid to your pancakes might seem odd, but I can promise you that it gives exceptional results in this recipe.

Sift the flour into a large bowl. Add the baking powder, salt and sugar and whisk together well.

In a smaller bowl, combine the aquafaba, vinegar, vanilla, melted vegan butter and nondairy milk. Mix well together; then pour slowly into the dry ingredients, stirring gently as you go, until no dry flour is visible. Do this by hand and not with an electric mixer, and do not overmix or beat really hard. Then, leave the batter to sit for 10 minutes. This is a really important step, so don't skip it. It will be quite thick at this stage.

The thickness of these pancakes is adjustable. You can make them thinner or thicker by adding or reducing the amount of milk added to the batter by a few tablespoons. A thinner batter makes thinner, less fluffy pancakes and a thicker batter makes taller, fluffier pancakes.

Heat a griddle or skillet over medium heat while the batter is resting. Brush the surface with a little neutral oil or vegan butter. Then pour or spoon the batter—using roughly ⅓ cup (80 ml) of batter for each one—onto the hot griddle. Cook for 3 to 4 minutes, or until you see small bubbles appear and the pancakes are puffy and starting to set around the edges. Flip very gently and cook for 2 to 3 minutes on the other side.

tips: *If you don't have a big griddle or pan, keep your oven on its lowest setting while you are cooking the pancakes. You can pop them in there to keep warm while you finish cooking them all.*

Once the pancake batter is on the griddle, switch them up a bit by dropping blueberries or chocolate chips gently on the top before flipping.

LOADED ZUCCHINI BREAKFAST CASSEROLE

yield: 6 servings

2 medium zucchini

1 tbsp (15 ml) olive oil or water

1 medium onion, chopped finely

16 oz (454 g) medium or firm tofu
(no need to press it)

2 cloves garlic

2 tsp (10 g) Dijon mustard

2 tbsp (16 g) arrowroot powder or
cornstarch

1 cup (240 ml) unsweetened
nondairy milk

1 tsp salt (reduce to ½ tsp if using
kala namak)

½ tsp freshly ground black pepper

2 tsp (about 4 g) dried mixed herbs,
such as herbes de Provence or
Italian seasoning

½ tsp red pepper flakes

¼ cup (28 g) nutritional yeast (see
note on page 49)

2 tbsp (30 ml) fresh lemon juice

1 tsp kala namak (optional; see note
on page 27)

1 cup (112 g) vegan cheese, divided
(optional)

1 generous handful of fresh parsley,
chopped

Make the most of your mornings with a comforting and hearty breakfast casserole. In this one, you will find golden flecks of hash browns, chunks of crusty bread and sweet sautéed zucchini all nestled in super-tasty custard. It's great for feeding a crowd and, as a bonus, the whole thing can be assembled the night before, if you need to. Just stash it away in the fridge and pop it into the oven the next morning while you enjoy your morning coffee.

Cut the zucchini in half lengthwise—then cut each half in half lengthwise again. Cut each stick into ½-inch (1.3-cm)-thick chunks.

In a large skillet, heat the olive oil or water over medium-high heat. Add the onion and zucchini chunks, and cook for about 10 minutes, or until the onion and zucchini are starting to turn golden. If using water to sauté, you will need to add a few more drops throughout the cooking process to prevent sticking. Remove from the heat and set aside.

In a blender, combine the tofu, garlic, mustard, arrowroot powder, nondairy milk, salt, black pepper, herbs, red pepper flakes, nutritional yeast, lemon juice and kala namak, if using. If you are using the optional vegan cheese, you can add half of that, too, if you wish, or just save it all for sprinkling on the top. Blend until smooth; then add the parsley and stir to incorporate.

(continued)

4 heaping cups (300 g) cubed plain, sourdough or flavored herby vegan bread (crusty bread that is slightly stale works best)

2 cups (260 g) hash browns (shredded or cubes), or the same quantity of fresh potatoes, peeled and cut into ⅛" (3-mm) cubes or grated with a food processor

Preheat the oven to 375°F (190°C). Then in a baking dish with at least a 2½-quart (2.5-L) capacity, layer half of the bread chunks across the bottom. Top with half of the zucchini mixture, and then scatter with 1 cup (130 g) of the hash browns. Cover the hash browns with most of the remaining bread, reserving a handful of chunks to scatter on the top later. Add the rest of the zucchini mixture; then pour the tofu mixture over that. It might sit on the top, but you can help it out by poking with a spoon or knife all over to give it channels to run down. Let the tofu mixture mostly seep in (it might take a few minutes), and then push the top down all over with a spatula to compact everything. Scatter the remaining hash browns over the top and poke in the reserved bread cubes so they are mostly sticking out and can get crispy. At this point, if you want to add the remaining ½ cup (56 g) of cheese, scatter it over the top.

Bake for 40 to 45 minutes, or until a knife inserted into the middle comes out almost clean. If your dish is very shallow, it will cook a little more quickly; if it is really deep, it might take a little longer.

Alternatively, if you want to cook the casserole the next morning, do not bake after assembly but cover with plastic wrap and stash it away in the fridge. For best results when doing this, if you are using potatoes rather than hash browns, make sure that they are all submerged so their color doesn't change overnight. Then, preheat the oven to 375°F (190°C) the next morning and bake, giving it an extra 5 minutes in the oven.

tip: *All sorts of veggies work well in this recipe. Cherry tomatoes, bell peppers, mushrooms and broccoli are good additions. Vegan sausages are also great in it.*

FEELIN' FRUITY YEAST BREAD

yield: 1 loaf

4 cups (500 g) all-purpose flour, plus more for dusting

1 tbsp (10 g) instant or fast-acting yeast

2 tsp (10 g) salt

1½ tsp (4 g) ground cinnamon

½ tsp ground nutmeg

½ tsp ground ginger

⅓ cup (67 g) cane or granulated white sugar

¼ cup (60 ml) melted and room-temperature vegan butter

¾ cup (180 ml) nondairy milk

½ cup + 2 tbsp (150 ml) lukewarm water (not hot)

⅔ cup (100 g) golden raisins

¼ cup (30 g) chopped dried apricots

¼ cup (30 g) dried cranberries

¼ cup (36 g) chopped pitted dates or figs

Oil or nonstick spray, for rising and bread pan

This plump and shiny, fruit-speckled yeast bread makes a lovely breakfast or afternoon treat. It might take a little time to make, but most of it is hands-off time, and it's so totally worth the effort involved when you present it glaze coated and glistening and watch everyone tuck in! It's really good fresh from the oven, spread with lots of vegan butter, but even better the next day when toasted or after a few days turned into French toast (page 23).

In the bowl of a stand mixer, stir together the flour, yeast, salt, cinnamon, nutmeg, ginger and sugar. Add the vegan butter, nondairy milk and water. Then attach the dough hook to the mixer and turn it on at medium-low speed. Knead for around 8 minutes. Alternatively, combine the ingredients in a large bowl and knead for about 15 minutes by hand. The dough needs to be completely smooth and elastic. Three to 4 minutes into kneading, turn off the mixer and give the dough a poke with your finger. It should be tacky but not overly sticky. If it's too sticky, add another couple tablespoons of flour; if it's dry, add a tablespoon (15 ml) or two (30 ml) of water. Be sure not to add too much extra flour, though, as it will affect the texture of your finished loaf.

Once the dough is smooth, add the dried fruit and carry on kneading for 1 to 2 minutes, until the fruit is incorporated evenly and the dough forms a ball. Grease a bowl with a drop of oil or some nonstick spray, add the dough ball and move it all around on all sides to coat the dough in the oil. Cover with a damp, clean dish towel (just run it under the tap for a few seconds, then wring it out) and leave on the kitchen counter until doubled. The time this takes will vary depending on how warm your kitchen is, but bear in mind that the longer it takes to rise, the more flavor there will be, so unless you are in a hurry, don't rush it by cranking up the heat or putting the bowl someplace very warm. Mine generally takes between 60 and 90 minutes to double and my kitchen is usually between 62 and 64°F (17 and 18°C).

(continued)

glaze

2 tbsp (25 g) cane or granulated white sugar

2 tbsp (30 ml) boiling water

While the dough rises, lightly oil a 9 x 5–inch (23 x 12.5–cm) loaf pan. Once the dough has doubled, scrape it gently onto a clean, lightly floured work surface. Shape into a loaf by using the heel of your hands to flatten it into a rectangle roughly the width of the bread pan. Fold the bottom third up and use the heel of your hand to push it down and seal it a bit. Next, fold the top third down (like an envelope) and push it down to seal it again. Then, fold the dough in half again and pinch it closed all the way along the seam. The idea is to make the surface of the dough as taut as you can. Gently turn under the ends if they look a little untidy, and then place in the prepared bread pan.

Rub a tiny bit of oil over the surface of the loaf to prevent sticking; then cover again with the damp dish towel and leave until the bread dough is nicely domed, and about 1 inch (2.5 cm) above the sides of the pan. It won't take as long this time, probably 30 to 40 minutes.

Meanwhile, preheat the oven to 400°F (200°C). Bake the loaf for 35 to 40 minutes. It should be nicely browned on top and coming away from the edges. Remove the pan from the oven and place on a cooling rack. If you knock on the bottom of the loaf, it should sound hollow.

Prepare the glaze. In a small bowl, stir the sugar into the boiling water until it has dissolved. Brush over the top of the warm loaf.

tips: Instead of shaping into a loaf, you could make buns. After the first rise, cut the dough into 8 evenly sized pieces, roll into balls and place on a baking sheet. Allow to double according to the directions—then bake for around 20 minutes.

Try drizzling frosting on the loaf instead of using the sugar glaze. Simply mix ½ cup (65 g) of powdered sugar with just enough water to make a thick but pourable glaze, then drizzle all over the loaf and allow to set.

CHOCOLATE-STUDDED PUMPKIN BREAD

yield: 10 slices

A little vegan butter, coconut oil or any other neutral oil, for pan

1¾ cups + 2 tbsp (240 g) whole wheat or all-purpose flour

¾ cup (150 g) coconut sugar

1 tsp baking soda

½ tsp baking powder

¼ tsp salt

1 tsp ground ginger

1 tsp ground cinnamon

¾ cup (135 g) vegan chocolate chips, plus a few more for sprinkling (see note)

½ cup (70 g) pumpkin seeds

1 cup + 2½ tbsp (260 g) pure pumpkin puree

½ cup (120 ml) unsweetened nondairy milk

1 tsp vanilla extract

It doesn't have to be fall to enjoy all things pumpkin. I like to make this quick, comfortingly spiced bread all year long. It's great for on-the-run breakfasts and is always popular in lunch boxes. Make it on those weekends when you are aching to bake but feeling a little virtuous. Everything in it is pretty healthy except for the chocolate chips, which I happen to think are very necessary because chocolate and pumpkin are best friends. You can easily omit or switch them out for pumpkin seeds, dried cranberries or raisins if you prefer, though.

Preheat the oven to 350°F (176°C) and grease a 9 x 5–inch (23 x 12.5–cm) loaf pan. Place a strip of parchment paper down the length of the pan with some overhang on each side to act as handles for removing the bread when it is baked.

In a large bowl, whisk together the flour, coconut sugar, baking soda, baking powder, salt, ginger and cinnamon. Then add the chocolate chips and pumpkin seeds.

In another bowl, mix together the pumpkin puree, nondairy milk and vanilla; then add them to the flour mixture and stir gently with a spatula. It is important not to overmix or beat the batter. Just keep going until you cannot see any more dry flour.

Spoon the batter into the prepared loaf pan. Smooth the top a little with a spatula and sprinkle with a few more chocolate chips for decoration.

Bake for 50 to 55 minutes, or until a toothpick inserted into the middle comes out clean. Remove from the pan using the paper "handles," peel off the parchment paper and allow to cool completely on a cooling rack before cutting.

Chocolate-Studded Pumpkin Bread keeps well for 4 to 5 days and also freezes well.

note: Chocolate is something we are all familiar with, but it tends to cause some confusion among new vegans. Chocolate in its natural form is vegan. It only becomes nonvegan when milk and milk fat are added. Look for dark chocolate and semisweet chocolate chips, and read their ingredients label carefully.

BERRY GOOD BREAKFAST CAKE

yield: 10 to 12 slices

Oil or vegan butter, for pan

1½ cups (173 g) spelt flour

2 tbsp (14 g) ground flaxseeds

1 cup (80 g) rolled oats, plus a few more for sprinkling on the top

¾ cup (150 g) coconut sugar

1½ tsp (6 g) baking soda

1 tbsp (12 g) baking powder

½ tsp ground cinnamon

½ tsp salt

1½ tbsp (23 ml) apple cider vinegar (see note)

½ cup (123 g) unsweetened applesauce

⅓ cup (80 g) plain, coconut or vanilla flavor vegan yogurt

1 tsp vanilla extract

1 cup (148 g) fresh blueberries, or 1 cup (155 g) frozen, plus a few to decorate the top

frosting

½ cup (130 g) powdered sugar

2 to 3 tbsp (30 to 45 g) plain, coconut or vanilla flavor vegan yogurt

Cake for breakfast is always a good thing! This one is stuffed full of healthy ingredients but still tastes like a treat, especially with the generous drizzle of sweet, tangy, yogurty frosting. Enjoy it fresh on the weekend—then eat the leftovers throughout the week.

Preheat the oven to 350°F (176°C). Grease the sides of an 8- or 9-inch (20.5- or 23-cm) round cake pan with a little oil or vegan butter and line the bottom with a circle of parchment paper.

In a large mixing bowl, combine the flour, ground flaxseeds, rolled oats, sugar, baking soda, baking powder, cinnamon and salt; then stir well.

In a separate bowl, combine the vinegar, applesauce, yogurt and vanilla and stir together.

Pour the wet ingredients into the dry and stir gently to combine. Don't overmix. The batter will be very thick. Fold the blueberries into the batter.

Spoon into the prepared cake pan and sprinkle with a few more oats and blueberries. Bake for about 40 minutes, or until a toothpick inserted into the middle of the cake comes out clean. Remove from the oven and leave in the pan for 10 minutes. Then remove the cake, peel off the baking parchment circle and allow to cool completely on a cooling rack.

Once the cake is cool, prepare the frosting: Put the powdered sugar in a small bowl. Add the yogurt gradually, a tablespoon (15 g) at a time, stirring really well between each addition to smooth it out. Stop when you have a thick but drizzlable consistency.

Drizzle all over the top of the cake, allowing some to spill over the sides.

Store, covered, in the fridge. It will keep for 4 to 5 days.

note: *You will find apple cider vinegar in most of my cake and sponge recipes. It is a must-have ingredient for any vegan baker. It might not seem like an obvious ingredient to add to a cake batter, but when combined with baking soda, a chemical reaction happens, making bubbles, creating air pockets and providing leavening. This, along with a little extra baking powder, replaces the leavening action that would otherwise be provided by eggs, so you get a light and fluffy sponge. Don't be tempted to skip it or you will end up with a flat cake!*

FULL ENGLISH FRITTATA

yield: 6 servings

12 oz (350 g) potatoes (roughly 3 medium), peeled and sliced into ⅛" to ³⁄₁₆" (3- to 4-mm) rounds

1 tsp salt

1½ cups (138 g) garbanzo flour (a.k.a. gram flour or besan)

1 tsp kala namak (see note on page 27) or regular salt

½ tsp freshly ground black pepper

1 tsp fresh rosemary, chopped finely

1½ cups (360 ml) water

1 tbsp (15 ml) olive oil

1 medium red onion, sliced into thin half-moons

2 large vegan sausages (about 6 oz [170 g] total), sliced into ⅛" to ³⁄₁₆" (3- to 4-mm) rounds

2 cloves garlic, chopped finely

5 white, cremini or baby bella mushrooms, sliced

4 slices vegan bacon or smoky tempeh, diced or crumbled

10 cherry or grape tomatoes, halved

Okay, I'm English, so a full English breakfast had to make it in here somewhere! This is a bit of a twist on a "full English," though, as it's in the form of a frittata. What's a frittata? It's kind of like a big, thick omelet that gets started off on the stovetop and then finished in the oven. In "full English" style, though, we are stuffing it with sausages, bacon, mushrooms, tomatoes, potatoes and an "eggy" batter. For a proper English breakfast experience, I recommend serving the frittata in great big wedges with a side of baked beans. No one will judge if they are from a can!

In a large saucepan, combine the potato rounds and salt, cover with boiling water, bring to a simmer and cook for 5 minutes. Then drain immediately and rinse in cold water. Set aside.

While the potatoes are cooking, in a bowl, combine the garbanzo flour, kala namak, pepper and rosemary, and gradually add the water, whisking as you go to work out any lumps. Set aside.

In an ovenproof skillet at least 10 inches (25.5 cm) in diameter and 2 inches (5 cm) deep, heat the oil over medium heat. Then add the onion and cook for about 10 minutes, or until it starts to brown. Add the sausage rounds, garlic, mushrooms and vegan bacon to the pan and cook for a further 2 to 3 minutes, moving everything around frequently, until they are just starting to turn golden on the edges.

Add the cooked potatoes to the pan, and stir and spread everything out so it is evenly distributed. Use a spatula to press everything down a bit so the top is fairly level.

Lower the heat to medium-low and add the garbanzo flour batter, moving the pan around a little from side to side so it distributes evenly. Then, scatter the halved tomatoes over the top and poke them in a bit with your finger or a spatula. Continue to cook on the stovetop for about 10 minutes, or until the sides are starting to firm up and it's beginning to bubble in places. While doing this, preheat the oven to 350°F (176°C).

Transfer the skillet to the oven and bake for 10 to 15 minutes, or until the batter is just firm to the touch. Please note that if your skillet is bigger than the recommended size, your frittata will be thinner, so it will cook more quickly. Remove from the oven and allow to rest for 10 minutes before turning out of the pan and slicing.

Leftovers will keep for up to 3 days in the fridge and are great warmed up or served cold.

ZESTY ORANGE OLIVE-OIL MUFFINS

yield: 6 muffins

¼ cup (60 ml) olive oil (extra-virgin gives the best flavor), plus more for the pan

1 cup (125 g) all-purpose flour

¼ cup (28 g) almond flour

1¼ tsp (5 g) baking powder

⅛ tsp baking soda

¼ tsp salt

¼ cup (50 g) granulated white or cane sugar

½ cup (120 ml) nondairy milk

Grated zest of 1 large orange

¼ cup + 2 tbsp (90 ml) fresh orange juice, divided

1½ tsp (8 ml) apple cider vinegar (see note on page 38)

1½ tsp (8 ml) vanilla extract

1 cup (130 g) powdered sugar

optional decoration

1 round orange slice, about ¹⁄₁₆" (2 mm) thick

2 tbsp (30 g) cane or granulated white sugar

Muffins for breakfast always feel like a bit of a splurge, and these even more so with their heady mixture of olive oil and orange. They are bright, fresh, fluffy and soft and won't weigh you down as your day gets started. They smell amazing when they are baking, too; and warm from the oven, they are the best treat to cozy up with on a chilly morning!

Preheat the oven to 425°F (218°C) and line 6 wells of a muffin pan with liners, or grease them with a little olive oil if you know you have a pan that releases well.

In a medium bowl, whisk together the all-purpose flour, almond flour, baking powder, baking soda, salt and sugar.

In another small bowl, combine the olive oil, nondairy milk, orange zest, ¼ cup (60 ml) of the orange juice, the vinegar and vanilla and stir well. Pour into the flour mixture and fold in. Do not beat it and do not overmix; simply stir enough that everything is just combined and you can't see any dry flour.

Divide the batter evenly among the prepared muffin wells (they will be quite full). Bake for 5 minutes. Then lower the oven temperature down to 375°F (190°C) and bake for 15 minutes more, or until a toothpick inserted into the middle of a muffin comes out clean. Remove from the pan and allow to cool completely on a cooling rack.

Once the muffins are cool, place the powdered sugar in a small bowl and gradually add the remaining orange juice, a few drops at a time, stirring really well between each addition, until you have a thick, drizzlable frosting. The maximum amount of orange juice you will need is 2 tablespoons (30 ml); it will probably be more like 1½ (23 ml). Resist adding more or it will end up too runny. If you accidentally add too much, you can add a little more powdered sugar to compensate.

If you want to make some little chewy orange pieces like the ones in my photograph, lay the orange round flat on a cutting board and, using the natural lines in the flesh as guides, cut into 6 equal wedge-shaped pieces. Lay them on a small parchment-lined baking sheet, sprinkle with sugar, turn over and sprinkle again, and then bake at 350°F (175°C) for 20 minutes, or until the sugar is melted and bubbly. Remove from the oven and allow to cool completely.

Drizzle the frosting over the muffins and stick one of the little orange pieces on the top of each muffin.

LEGIT ENGLISH MUFFINS

yield: 8 muffins

3 cups (375 g) all-purpose unbleached white flour, plus more for dusting

½ tsp salt

2 tsp (8 g) cane or granulated white sugar

2 tsp (7 g) instant or fast-acting yeast

1½ tsp (6 g) baking soda

2 tbsp (30 ml) melted and room-temperature refined coconut oil or vegan butter

¾ cup + 1 tbsp + 1 tsp (200 ml) tepid water (just slightly warm to touch, not hot)

Oil, for rising

Cornmeal, for dusting

Make your own English muffins once and you will never go back to store-bought. They are so much better—plus the whole process of making them is cathartic. There is nothing quite like watching them puff up like little clouds while they cook. They are amazing while still hot straight from the griddle, but also super good toasted. Split them open with a fork or your fingers rather than with a knife, which gives too smooth a surface. Then toast and allow the vegan butter and jam to pool in their many nooks and crannies. Be sure to save some to use as a vehicle for my amazing Tofu Benny (page 47), too!

If you have a stand mixer with a dough hook, place all the ingredients, except the oil and cornmeal, in the bowl. Mix on low speed, using the hook attachment. Alternatively, in a large bowl, combine all the ingredients, except the oil and cornmeal; then stir briefly to mix everything before turning out onto a lightly floured surface and kneading by hand. After a few minutes of kneading, if the dough is too sticky, add a few tablespoons of flour, 1 tablespoon (8 g) at a time, giving it a chance to knead in between additions, until the dough is just very slightly tacky to the touch but not sticky. If it feels really dry and isn't tacky at all, add another tablespoon (15 ml) or two (30 ml) of water very gradually, kneading between additions until it becomes *just* tacky. Carry on kneading for 7 to 10 minutes in the mixer, or about 15 minutes by hand, until the dough is really smooth and elastic.

Once smooth and elastic, place in a large, lightly oiled bowl and cover with a clean, damp dish towel (I run one under the tap for a few seconds and then wring it out well before placing over the bowl). Leave in a draft-free area until it has doubled in size (the time this takes will vary. For me it usually takes 60 to 90 minutes, but it could take longer).

Line a large baking sheet with parchment paper and sprinkle it generously with cornmeal.

Once the dough has approximately doubled in size, turn it out onto a lightly floured surface and roll it out with a rolling pin until it is about 1 inch (2.5 cm) thick. Make sure it is even all over.

(continued)

Use a round cookie cutter about 3 inches (7.5 cm) in diameter to cut rounds and place them on the prepared baking sheet. Be sure to cut carefully and get as many as you can out of the first batch of rolled dough because the muffins from the first batch are always slightly better than those made with the remaining dough. When you have cut as many as you can, ball up the remaining dough and reroll it. Then cut out the remaining muffins.

Sprinkle the tops of the muffins with more cornmeal, cover (using the same damp dish towel as earlier) and leave again until almost doubled in size. It won't take as long this time, usually 30 to 40 minutes. They should be really puffy and light.

If you have a griddle, heat it over medium-low heat. If you have an electric griddle, set it at 325°F (162°C). If you don't have a griddle, you can use a heavy skillet instead over medium-low heat.

When the griddle is to temperature, place as many muffins as will fit comfortably—with sufficient room to turn them easily—*very* gently on the griddle. It's important to be as gentle as possible because you don't want to knock any of the air out of them. Keep any remaining uncooked muffins under the damp dish towel while you are cooking the first batch.

Cook for 5 to 7 minutes, or until beautifully golden on the bottom; then very gently turn them over and cook for another 5 to 7 minutes. Remove from the pan and place on a cooling rack. Cook the remaining muffins.

Cooked English muffins can be frozen in a sealed container or freezer bag for up to 2 months. Defrost for a few hours or overnight before using.

TOFU BENNY WITH "HOLLANDAISE" SAUCE

yield: 2 large or 4 small servings

"hollandaise" sauce

¼ cup (43 g) blanched whole almonds

1 tbsp (7 g) nutritional yeast (see note)

1 tbsp (15 ml) white wine vinegar

1½ tbsp (23 ml) fresh lemon juice

2 tbsp (30 g) vegan butter

½ cup (120 ml) unsweetened nondairy milk

Pinch of ground turmeric (optional, for color only)

¼ tsp salt

⅛ tsp ground white pepper (black is okay, but you might see the flecks in the sauce)

⅛ tsp garlic powder

¼ tsp smoked paprika

1 medium sweet potato with a diameter about the same as an English muffin

1 tbsp (15 ml) olive oil, plus more for brushing

¼ tsp salt, divided

¼ tsp freshly ground black pepper, divided

3 cloves garlic, chopped finely

3 cups packed (100 g) spinach, rinsed well and drained

Mornings have just become more magical, because guess what? You don't need eggs to make a great Benny! In this recipe, I poach medium-firm tofu in water just as one would an egg. The texture ends up uncannily similar to an egg white. Then, it's layered with a thick slice of tender, pan-roasted sweet potato, a generous pile of sautéed garlicky spinach and a big drizzle of super-easy, creamy, tangy, blender "hollandaise." It's decadent, it's indulgent and it makes a wonderful brunch offering. Once you've mastered this version, you can explore and get creative. A large roasted portobello mushroom would work incredibly well in place of the sweet potato, and crispy vegan bacon or tempeh squeezed into those layers would be amazing too!

Prepare the "hollandaise." In a high-powered blender, combine all the sauce ingredients and blend until completely smooth. Alternatively, soak the almonds in either cold water overnight or boiling water for 30 minutes before blending everything together in a standard blender. Transfer the sauce to a small saucepan and set aside.

Heat a heavy-bottomed skillet over medium heat, or heat an indoor electric grill to medium. Peel the sweet potato and cut four ½-inch (1.3-cm)-thick slices from the middle area so they end up roughly the same diameter. Brush the rounds with a little olive oil before placing in the hot pan. Season the tops with a pinch of salt and black pepper, and then let the slices cook without moving for 5 to 7 minutes. Flip, seasoning the other side as before, and cook for a further 5 to 7 minutes, or until they are fork-tender. If they start getting a little too caramelized, turn the heat to low.

Meanwhile, in a large skillet, heat the tablespoon (15 ml) of olive oil over medium heat. Add the garlic and cook for 1 to 2 minutes; then add the spinach. It will seem like a lot and will be a struggle to get it all in the pan, but it will wilt down to a much more manageable amount in a few minutes. Season the spinach with a pinch of salt and pepper. Give it a stir every few minutes. Once it has wilted down completely, turn off the heat but leave the skillet on the burner so it keeps warm.

(continued)

16 oz (454 g) medium-firm tofu (a block that is rectangular rather than square works best; no need to press it)

2 Legit English Muffins (page 45)

2 pinches of kala namak (optional; see note on page 27)

Smoked paprika (optional)

Bring a kettle of water to a boil and pour it into a wide, shallow skillet to a depth of about 2 inches (5 cm). Place over medium heat and allow to gently simmer. Meanwhile, drain the tofu and cut it into 4 evenly sized pieces: First, cut horizontally through the middle to make 2 long pieces, and then cut each of those pieces in half to make 4 squares. If you want to be fancy, you can use a cookie cutter to cut rounds. Gently lower the pieces of tofu into the simmering water with the help of a spatula. Leave them to simmer for 3 minutes, and then remove very carefully. They will be quite fragile. Drain on a sheet of paper towel.

While the tofu is simmering, warm the hollandaise gently over low heat. Split the English muffins and toast them until golden. If the sauce gets a little thick, you can add a few drops of water to thin it.

To plate, place one-quarter of the spinach on each muffin half, followed by a sweet potato round, followed by a piece of tofu. Sprinkle the tofu with a pinch of kala namak (if using) for an "eggy" flavor; then drizzle the stacks with hollandaise sauce and serve. A sprinkle of smoked paprika on the top of each looks really nice!

tip: You can buy ready-blanched almonds, but if you have raw ones at home, you can easily blanch them yourself. Here's how:

Put the almonds in a small bowl. Cover them with boiling water and leave for 5 minutes, before draining. Pick up an almond and hold it between two fingers at the rounded end. Squeeze and the almond will pop out of the skin.

note: Nutritional yeast is an ingredient that I use often in my recipes, and it is available in most grocery stores, health food stores and also from online retailers, such as Amazon. It is very different to the yeast you use to make bread or beer, so don't try replacing it with that. In larger amounts, it gives a lovely cheesy flavor and is perfect for making such things as mac and cheese (page 84), but when used in small amounts it adds a savory depth of flavor or a buttery flavor, such as in this recipe.

CRISPY CORNMEAL WAFFLES WITH MAPLE-ROASTED CHERRY TOMATOES

yield: 6 medium waffles

topping

3 cups (450 g) cherry or grape tomatoes

2 tsp (10 ml) olive oil

2 tsp (10 ml) pure maple syrup, plus more for serving

⅛ tsp salt

⅛ tsp freshly ground pepper

waffles

1 cup (116 g) corn flour (not to be confused with cornstarch) or fine cornmeal

½ cup (63 g) all-purpose flour

1 tbsp (12 g) baking powder

½ tsp salt

1 tbsp (12 g) cane or granulated white sugar

2 tbsp (14 g) ground flaxseeds

3 tbsp (45 ml) olive oil

1 cup (240 ml) unsweetened nondairy milk

Oil or vegan butter, for waffle iron

There are zero good reasons why you shouldn't change up the way you waffle, and a stack of crispy on the outside, super-fluffy-on-the-inside cornmeal waffles with a tumble of sticky, sweet cherry tomatoes and a drizzle of maple syrup is a great place to start. They are the perfect mix of sweet and savory, but if you'd rather a more traditional brunch experience, the waffles work really well with regular sweet toppings, too, and are amazing with the cherry sauce from my Black Forest Breakfast Crepes (page 17). If you don't have a waffle maker, this recipe makes amazingly fluffy pancakes, too!

Prepare the topping. Preheat the oven to 400°F (200°C) and line a small baking sheet with parchment paper.

Put the tomatoes into a bowl and add the olive oil, maple syrup, salt and pepper. Stir to coat, and then transfer to the prepared baking sheet. Roast for 25 to 30 minutes or until sticky and slightly caramelized. Then lower the oven temperature to its lowest setting and leave them in there until you have finished making the waffles.

Prepare the waffles. In a bowl, whisk together the corn flour, all-purpose flour, baking powder, salt, sugar and ground flaxseeds.

In a small bowl or jug, mix the olive oil with the nondairy milk, and then pour into the flour mixture. Whisk until combined. Do not overmix; stop as soon as all the dry flour is absorbed and most of the lumps are gone. Leave to sit for 10 minutes. It will be very thick.

While the batter is resting, preheat a waffle iron according to the manufacturer's instructions. Once the waffle iron is hot, grease it with oil or vegan butter. Allow it to come to temperature again, if necessary, and then spoon in the batter. The amount you need will depend on the size of your waffle iron, but let it go almost to the edges. Close and allow to cook for 3 to 5 minutes, or until steam has stopped coming out of the sides of the waffle iron. By then, they should be really crisp and it should open easily with the waffles intact.

As you cook the waffles, transfer them to a baking sheet and allow to keep warm in the oven on its lowest setting until you have finished the entire batch.

Serve the waffles with the cherry tomatoes on top and a drizzle of maple syrup.

GO-TO TOFU SCRAMBLE

yield: 3 or 4 servings

2 tsp (10 ml) olive oil or water

1 medium onion, chopped finely

1 large poblano pepper, ribs and seeds removed, chopped into small pieces

4 cloves garlic, chopped finely

12 oz (350 g) medium-firm tofu (no need to press it)

½ tsp kala namak (see note on page 27) or regular salt, plus more to taste

Freshly ground black pepper

6 tbsp (90 ml) unsweetened nondairy milk of choice

Tofu scramble is the perfect breakfast comfort food and makes a great alternative to scrambled eggs, which were one of my favorite breakfasts before I became vegan. Kala namak gives the tofu a real "eggy" flavor and I love to add some poblano pepper for a gentle touch of spice. By using medium-firm tofu and adding a splash of nondairy milk, you get a really moist, fluffy and soft scramble that is hearty, satisfying and so good tumbled over a thick wedge of warm "buttery" toast. Make it a more substantial meal by serving a veggie sausage, grilled tomatoes and sautéed mushrooms alongside.

In a skillet over medium heat, heat the oil or water. Sauté the onion for about 5 minutes, or until translucent. If using water to sauté, add a little more as needed throughout the cooking process to prevent sticking.

Add the chopped poblano pepper and garlic and continue to cook, stirring frequently, for 3 to 4 minutes, or until the poblano is just tender.

Meanwhile, drain the tofu. Then crumble it into little pieces with your fingers and add it to the pan once the onion has started to caramelize and the poblano is beginning to soften.

Add the kala namak for an "eggy" flavor, or use regular salt, as well as plenty of freshly ground black pepper, and continue to cook, stirring frequently, for 2 to 3 minutes more.

Just before serving, pour in the nondairy milk. It may seem like a strange addition, but it makes the tofu really moist, like the texture of scrambled egg. Keep stirring for another 1 to 2 minutes, or until almost all of the liquid has been absorbed, then have a quick taste and adjust the seasoning, if necessary.

tip: *Poblano peppers are only mildly spicy, but if you would rather have no heat at all, use a green bell pepper instead.*

PEAR-FECT BAKED OATMEAL

yield: 6 servings

2¾ cups (248 g) rolled oats

½ cup (100 g) cane or granulated white sugar

½ cup (55 g) roughly chopped or slivered almonds, plus more for scattering

2 tbsp (14 g) ground flaxseeds

1½ tsp (6 g) baking powder

2 tsp (5 g) ground cinnamon

½ tsp ground ginger

½ tsp salt

1½ cups (360 ml) unsweetened nondairy milk

¼ cup + 1 tbsp (80 g) almond butter, plus more for drizzling

1 tbsp (15 ml) vanilla extract

3 ripe pears

Upgrade your boring bowl of oatmeal for a hearty baked version! This one is filled with wholesome oats and studded with sliced, juicy pear and crunchy chopped almonds. It's kind of like a cross between cake and a soft oaty bar. It's fancy enough to serve for brunch and easy enough to make ahead for super-quick breakfasts throughout the week. I love to serve it warm, cut into squares and drizzled with drippy almond butter and maple syrup!

Preheat the oven to 375°F (190°C) and line an 8-inch (20.5-cm) square baking dish with parchment paper.

In a bowl, combine the oats, sugar, almonds, ground flaxseeds, baking powder, cinnamon, ginger and salt, and stir well.

In a separate bowl, stir together the nondairy milk, almond butter and vanilla. If your almond butter is really drippy, you can do this by hand; but if it's stiffer, it will be easier to put it in a blender and blend for 10 to 20 seconds, or until smooth.

Peel the pears, cut them in half and use a teaspoon or melon baller to remove the cores. Cut 2 of the pears into ½-inch (1.3-cm) cubes and the remaining pear into slices.

Pour the wet ingredients into the dry and stir them together well. Add the chopped pears and stir to incorporate. Spoon into the prepared dish and press down all over to smooth out the top. Arrange the pear slices on the top and sprinkle with a few more almonds; then bake for 35 to 40 minutes, or until firmed up and a little crusty around the edges.

Serve immediately or allow to cool in the pan. Store wrapped or in an airtight container in the fridge for up to 5 days. This can be eaten warm or cold. Reheat individual slices in the microwave for 20 to 30 seconds.

tip: *You can switch this up by using any other fruit you like. Apples work well, as do berries.*

indulge yourself

And now to the main event! When you need a hearty, satisfying meal, this is the place to come.

Satisfy your savory comfort food cravings in style with my take on your feel-good family favorites. We're talking drool-worthy "meatballs," lasagna, stew and dumplings, creamy risotto, mac and "cheese" and so much more. They are all ready and waiting to be made, enjoyed and shared with those you love.

You won't find any meat or dairy products, but you will find big flavor. These recipes are all real crowd-pleasers, and whether you or your guests are vegan or not, I can guarantee that they will be enjoyed by all.

SPEEDY MUSHROOM STROGANOFF

yield: 4 servings

5 large portobello mushrooms

2 tbsp (30 ml) mild oil of choice (optional) or water

1½ cups (360 ml) water

½ cup (120 g) cashew butter

1 medium onion, finely chopped

5 cloves garlic, finely chopped

5 tbsp (75 ml) brandy or cognac (optional but recommended)

1 tbsp + 1 tsp (20 g) Dijon mustard

1 slightly heaping tsp smoked or regular paprika

2½ tbsp (38 ml) white wine vinegar or apple cider vinegar

1¼ tsp (6 g) salt

¾ tsp freshly ground black pepper

3 tbsp (12 g) fresh dill or parsley, chopped finely

Pasta, rice, potatoes or polenta, for serving

tip: *Marsala, bourbon, whiskey or dry white wine all make great alternatives to the brandy.*

Comfort food at its finest! This is a dinner party–worthy meal that's ready in less than 30 minutes, is super easy to make and tastes really decadent. My spin on stroganoff, though, is a little untraditional. I like to use cashew butter instead of vegan sour cream because it adds more flavor and makes a richer, creamier sauce. I also like to add a dash of brandy and a scattering of fresh dill. Just a little of both make all the difference. Brandy adds fantastic depth of flavor, and dill, although my least favorite herb and one I hardly ever use, just works fantastically in this recipe. Serve over pasta, mashed potato, rice or polenta. Anything that's a suitable vehicle to soak up that delicious creamy sauce!

Wipe the mushrooms clean with paper towels, and then gently remove the stems. Set the stems aside; do not discard. Cut each mushroom into ½-inch (1.3-cm)-thick slices. You can cut them in half again to make the pieces smaller or leave them large.

In a large skillet, heat the oil over high heat. Add the mushrooms and sear for about 2 minutes on each side until they are a deep, golden brown. If you use a good nonstick skillet, you can omit the oil to make the recipe oil-free or use a few tablespoons of water instead of the oil, adding a little more as necessary while the mushrooms cook to prevent them from sticking. You might need to cook them in batches, depending on the size of your skillet. Transfer them to a plate and set aside when done.

In a blender or food processor, combine the mushroom stems, water and cashew butter and blend until completely smooth. It won't look appetizing at this stage, but don't worry—everything will come together soon. Set aside.

Place the pan you seared the mushrooms in over medium heat, and sauté the onion for about 10 minutes, or until golden. Add the garlic and cook for a further minute or two; then add the brandy (if using). It will sizzle. Stir the mixture around, scraping up any brown residue from the bottom of the pan, and allow the brandy to absorb into the onion.

Lower the heat to medium-low and add the mushroom stem mixture as well as the mustard, paprika, vinegar, salt and pepper. Stir until everything is creamy and combined. If it appears too thick, add a few drops of water to thin, and then add the seared mushrooms back to the pan. Allow to warm through for a few minutes and add the dill immediately before serving. Serve over pasta, rice, potatoes or polenta.

SOUL-WARMING STEW AND DUMPLINGS

yield: 6 to 8 servings

1 tbsp (15 ml) olive oil

1 medium onion, chopped finely

3 medium carrots, cut into ½" (1.3-cm) cubes

2 celery ribs, finely chopped

4 cloves garlic, finely chopped

2 large white potatoes (about 21 oz [600 g] total), peeled and cut into ½" (1.3-cm) cubes

1 green bell pepper, seeded and cut into ½" (1.3-cm) cubes

4 cups (550 g) cubed rutabaga, turnip or more carrot and potato (½" [1.3-cm]) cubes

5.5 oz (156 g) tomato paste

1 cup (192 g) dried red lentils (not green or brown)

1 large bay leaf

1 qt (1 L) vegetable or mushroom stock

1 qt (1 L) water

¼ cup (60 ml) soy sauce, tamari or coconut aminos (see note)

1½ tsp (2 g) dried thyme

1 tsp salt, plus more to taste

¾ tsp freshly ground black pepper

Is there anything more comforting than a giant pot of fragrant stew bubbling away on the stovetop? It was always one of my favorite dinners while growing up, and in this recipe I think I capture that rich, hearty depth of flavor that you expect in a slow-cooked stew but don't always get when they are meat-free. As for the dumplings, they are perfect, light, fluffy, buttery-tasting clouds, way better than any I had before I was vegan and not stodgy in the slightest. The bonus when making this is the amazing smell that wafts through the house as it gently simmers itself to perfection!

In a large soup pot, heat the olive oil over medium heat. Add the onion, carrots and celery and sauté for 5 minutes, or until the onion is translucent. Add the garlic, potatoes, bell pepper and rutabaga, followed by the tomato paste. Stir together well and then tip in the lentils, bay leaf, stock, water, soy sauce, thyme, salt and black pepper.

Bring to a simmer. Then lower the heat to medium-low and continue to cook for 1 hour, stirring occasionally and making sure to scrape the bottom of the pan well. By this time, the vegetables should be tender and the stew should have thickened nicely. At this point you can continue with the recipe, or you can keep it simmering over very low heat for up to 3 hours, making sure to stir occasionally.

(continued)

dumplings

1 cup (125 g) all-purpose flour

2 tsp (8 g) baking powder

2 tbsp (14 g) nutritional yeast (see note on page 49)

¼ tsp salt

Pinch of freshly ground black pepper

2 tbsp (30 g) very cold vegan butter (page 188)

About ½ cup (120 ml) unsweetened nondairy milk

When you are almost ready to serve, check the seasoning and adjust as necessary. Next prepare the dumplings. In a small bowl, stir together the flour, baking powder, nutritional yeast, salt and black pepper; then add the cold butter. Cut or rub it in with a fork or the tips of your fingers until it looks like coarse bread crumbs. Gradually add the nondairy milk while stirring until a soft, sticky dough is formed. You might not need all of the milk. Drop the dough by the tablespoonful (15 g) onto the top of the stew, leaving plenty of room between each dumpling, because they will more than double in size. Then use a spoon to gently scoop up some stew liquid and pour a little over the top of each one. Cover the pot and let the dumplings steam for 15 to 20 minutes, or until light, puffy and cloudlike.

Serve the stew in bowls, topped with the dumplings.

The stew will keep in the fridge for up to 5 days and will reheat really well in a microwave or on the stovetop. The dumplings get a little less fluffy when reheated, but are still good.

note: Soy sauce or tamari might seem an odd ingredient to add here, but it is my secret weapon in recipes that need rich, tasty sauces or gravies. It works incredibly well in vegan versions of recipes that would usually contain meat, giving a real "meaty," rich depth of flavor. Don't even think about skipping it, although coconut aminos can be used instead if you don't consume soy products.

HEARTY PORTOBELLO AND ALE POT PIE

yield: 5 or 6 servings

filling

6 large portobello mushrooms

4 tsp (20 ml) olive oil, divided

1 onion, chopped finely

2 medium carrots, sliced

2 celery ribs, chopped finely

4 large cloves garlic, chopped finely

12 small shallots or baby onions, peeled and left whole

3 tbsp (24 g) arrowroot powder or cornstarch

2 cups (480 ml) ale (darker varieties give the best flavor)

1 tbsp (16 g) whole-grain mustard

¼ cup (60 g) tomato paste

¼ cup (60 ml) tamari or soy sauce (see note on page 62)

1 tbsp (12 g) cane or granulated white sugar

1 tsp salt

¼ tsp freshly ground black pepper

"egg" wash

3 tbsp (45 ml) nondairy milk

1 tbsp (15 ml) pure maple syrup

1 tbsp (15 ml) mildly flavored oil

Pies are made for sharing with those you love and are the epitome of comfort food. While they are a little more labor intensive than your average meal, that contrast between crisp pastry and delicious filling is so worth it, and I can guarantee that your friends and family will appreciate your efforts when they are tucking into this one. Juicy mushrooms and sweet baby onions smothered in the most incredible gravy and topped with a crispy, buttery pastry crust make it pretty epic. That moment when you break through the pastry to reveal the meaty mushrooms and the thick, rich, ale-infused gravy ... let's just say you should be prepared to swoon.

Prepare the filling. Wipe the portobello mushrooms clean; then cut them in half and cut each half into 1-inch (2.5-cm)-thick slices. In a large skillet, heat 2 teaspoons (10 ml) of the olive oil over medium heat. Add the mushrooms and sauté for about 10 minutes, making sure to brown each piece on both sides. Once browned, remove from the pan and set aside.

Use the same pan to heat the remaining 2 teaspoons (10 ml) of olive oil over medium heat. Then add the onion, carrots and celery. Cook, stirring frequently, for about 5 minutes, or until the onion is translucent; then add the garlic and shallots. Continue to cook until everything is starting to caramelize and go golden, around 15 minutes.

Stir in the arrowroot powder really well so everything is coated, and then pour in the ale and stir well again. Add the mustard, tomato paste, tamari, sugar, salt and pepper and stir. Then simmer for 10 to 15 minutes, or until the shallots are just fork-tender and the gravy is nice and thick.

Remove from the heat, add the cooked mushroom slices, stir to distribute and allow to cool.

Preheat the oven to 425°F (218°C). Meanwhile, in a small bowl, prepare the "egg" wash by whisking the nondairy milk, maple syrup and oil together.

(continued)

crust

2 cups (250 g) all-purpose flour, plus more for dusting

½ tsp fine salt

½ cup (110 g) very cold, hard vegan butter

About 6 tbsp (90 ml) ice-cold water

Prepare the crust. In a large bowl, combine the flour and salt and stir well. Then add the vegan butter. Cut the butter into the flour, or rub it in with your fingertips, until any lumps of butter have gone and the flour looks like coarse bread crumbs.

Add the cold water gradually, a tablespoon (15 ml) at a time, stirring with a knife, until a dough starts to form. Bring it together with your hands and shape gently into a ball. The amount of water needed will vary. You might need more; you might need less.

Dust a clean work surface with flour; then roll the pastry so it is large enough to cover the top of a large, roughly 10-inch (25.5-cm)-wide by 3-inch (7.5-cm)-deep pie dish, skillet or casserole. The pastry should be about an inch (2.5 cm) wider than the dish all the way around.

Spoon the cold portobello filling into the dish and then gently lay the pastry over it. Crimp the edges to seal, brush gently all over with the "egg" wash and then cut a 1-inch (2.5-cm)-long slit in the middle of the pastry to allow steam to escape from the pie.

Place on a baking sheet and bake for around 40 minutes, or until the pastry is crispy and golden.

tips: The filling for the pie can be made up to 3 days in advance and stored in the refrigerator until needed.

For a lighter version, follow the directions for the pie filling but simmer long enough for the shallots to become completely tender. Add the mushrooms, allow to warm through and then serve without a pastry crust. It's perfect with some mashed or roasted potatoes and steamed vegetables.

MOM'S SPAGHETTI AND "MEATBALLS"

yield: 5 or 6 servings

meatballs

1 medium onion, divided

2 cups (480 g) canned chickpeas, drained and rinsed

5 cloves garlic

¼ cup (60 ml) soy sauce or tamari (see note on page 62)

¼ cup (28 g) nutritional yeast (see note on page 49)

¼ cup (60 g) tomato ketchup

1 tsp dried oregano

1 tsp dried thyme

¾ tsp freshly ground black pepper

1 cup (117 g) shelled walnuts or pecans, chopped finely

1¾ cups (210 g) vital wheat gluten (see note)

¼ to ½ cup (60 to 120 ml) vegetable stock (optional)

Flour (any will do), for kneading (optional)

2 tsp (10 ml) oil (any will do), for pan

This recipe involves everything the whole family wants and needs: a big ol' plate of spaghetti, lots of rich marinara sauce and big, super tasty meatballs that are actually tender, robust and "meaty" despite being vegan. I promise that they will not disintegrate into the sauce as many vegan meatballs do. This is a cozy, timeless, feel-good meal that is set to become your favorite family-night dinner.

To prepare the meatballs, peel the onion and cut it in half. Put half of the onion into the bowl of a food processor and set the other half aside. Add the chickpeas, garlic, soy sauce, nutritional yeast, tomato ketchup, oregano, thyme and pepper to the food processor. Then process until it is all a smooth paste, stopping the food processor once to scrape down the sides.

Chop the reserved onion half finely and add it to the puree in the food processor along with the nuts. Pulse 3 or 4 times to distribute; then remove the blade and scrape the mixture into the bowl of a stand mixer fitted with the dough hook, or into a large mixing bowl.

Add the vital wheat gluten to the bowl and mix until most of it is combined. If it is very dry and won't combine properly, you will need to add some of the stock to make a stiffish dough that is slightly tacky but not wet. I used ¼ cup (60 ml), but it will vary each time. You might need up to ½ cup (120 ml), possibly a few tablespoons more. Add it very gradually and keep mixing between additions. If you are not using a stand mixer, it will probably be easier to use your hands to knead in the liquid.

Knead the meatball dough on a medium speed for 5 minutes in a stand mixer, or turn it out onto a lightly floured surface and knead for 8 minutes if doing it by hand. Once kneaded, leave it to rest in the bowl for 10 minutes.

While it is resting, preheat the oven to 400°F (200°C) and line a large baking sheet with parchment paper. Rub a little oil over the parchment paper to prevent sticking.

Using about 2 tablespoons (30 g) of mixture for each, roll the dough into tight balls and place them on the prepared baking sheet, making sure they don't touch. Bake for 30 to 35 minutes, turning them at about the 15-minute point. They should develop a nice crusty exterior but have some give if you squeeze them.

See photo on page 8.

marinara

1 tbsp (15 ml) olive oil or water

1 medium onion, finely chopped

4 cloves garlic, finely chopped

1 (28-oz [793-g]) can crushed tomatoes or passata

¼ cup (28 g) nutritional yeast (see note on page 49)

1 tsp dried oregano

1 tsp dried basil

2 tsp (10 g) salt, plus more to taste

¼ tsp freshly ground black pepper

1 tbsp (12 g) cane or granulated white sugar

1½ cups (360 ml) water

1 lb (454 g) dried spaghetti

to serve

Cheesy Brazil Nut "Parm" (page 191; optional)

There's No Such Thing as Too Much Garlic Bread (page 125; optional)

While the meatballs are cooking, prepare the marinara. In a large, wide sauté pan over medium heat, heat the olive oil, and then sauté the onion for about 5 minutes, or until translucent. Alternatively, use a little water to sauté, to make the recipe oil-free. Add the garlic and continue to cook, stirring frequently, for another 2 minutes. Transfer to a blender along with all the other marinara ingredients. Blend until completely smooth; then return to the pan. Bring to a gentle simmer, lower the heat to low and continue to cook for 30 minutes, or until rich and thick. Check the seasoning and add more to taste, if necessary.

Drop the cooked meatballs gently into the sauce 10 to 15 minutes before serving.

Bring a large pot of water to a boil and cook the spaghetti according to the directions on the package. Drain, return to the pot and spoon in enough marinara sauce to coat the spaghetti. Toss well and then place the spaghetti on individual dinner plates or in bowls. Top with the meatballs and some more sauce.

Serve with Cheesy Brazil Nut "Parm" or grated vegan cheese and some of my There's No Such Thing as Too Much Garlic Bread.

tip: Once baked, the meatballs can be cooled and will keep for 4 to 5 days in the fridge or in the freezer for up to 3 months.

note: Vital wheat gluten, sometimes known as wheat gluten or wheat protein, is basically flour that has been hydrated to activate the gluten and then processed to remove everything but the gluten. In vegan recipes, it is used to give a very realistic "meaty" texture and is the main ingredient in seitan (a popular vegan meat substitute), but it can also be used as a dough improver in bread recipes. It is becoming increasingly common at grocery stores and health food stores, but if you have trouble finding it, it's easy to get from online retailers, such as Amazon.

RICH AND SAUCY BOLOGNESE

yield: 4½ cups (1.1 L)

2 tsp (10 ml) olive oil or water

1 medium onion, chopped finely

1 medium carrot, cut into ¼" (6-mm) cubes

1 medium celery rib, chopped finely

4 cloves garlic, chopped finely

1 small eggplant, cut into ¼" (6-mm) cubes

¾ cup (180 ml) red wine or vegetable stock

½ cup (100 g) dried green lentils

¼ cup (45 g) dried red lentils

3 tbsp (45 g) tomato paste

14 oz (400 g) crushed canned tomatoes or passata

½ tsp dried rosemary

½ tsp dried oregano

½ tsp dried thyme

⅛ tsp smoked paprika

3 tbsp (21 g) nutritional yeast (see note on page 49)

2 tbsp (30 ml) soy sauce or tamari (see note on page 62)

1 tbsp (12 g) cane or granulated white sugar

1 cup (240 ml) vegetable stock or water

1 tsp salt, plus more to taste

½ tsp freshly ground black pepper, plus more to taste

To me, mastering a great spag bol was a priority when I became vegan because it's one of my favorite midweek dinners. It also happens to be comfort in a bowl. Who doesn't love a pile of spaghetti tossed in hearty, "meaty" sauce? My version is rich and complex with lots of layers of flavor, and every little ingredient, along with the slow cooking, does its bit in making that happen. The wine, although not essential, really adds great depth of flavor, so I highly recommend using it if you can. Serve this sauce in the traditional way, over al dente spaghetti, fettuccine or pappardelle with a heavy sprinkling of my Cheesy Brazil Nut "Parm" (page 191) and a side of my garlic bread (page 125).

In a large sauté pan, heat the olive oil or a couple tablespoons (30 ml) of water (for oil-free cooking) over medium heat. Add the onion, carrot and celery and cook for 6 to 7 minutes, or until the onion is translucent and just starting to turn golden. If using water to sauté, you will need to add a little more throughout the cooking process to prevent sticking.

Add the garlic and eggplant and continue to cook for 3 to 4 minutes; then add the red wine (if you are replacing wine with stock, wait to add the stock until you add the other ingredients). Keep stirring until it has been absorbed/evaporated. Then add all the other ingredients. Stir really well and allow to come to a simmer. Then lower the heat to low and cook for at least 40 to 50 minutes, or until the lentils are tender, but you can leave it on really low for up to about 90 minutes. Be sure to stir it occasionally and check the texture. If it starts to dry out, add a little more water or stock to loosen it up again.

Taste and adjust the seasoning as necessary before serving.

The sauce will keep for 5 to 6 days in the fridge and also freezes well.

tip: *This sauce is great when used in place of the marinara in my lasagna recipe (page 81).*

"I CAN'T BELIEVE IT'S VEGAN" ROASTED GARLIC ALFREDO

yield: 5 servings

1 tsp olive oil

2 large whole heads garlic

½ cup (70 g) raw cashews (soaked in boiling water for 15 minutes if you don't have a high-powered blender, then drained)

½ packed cup (50 g) ground almonds or almond meal

½ cup (56 g) nutritional yeast (see note on page 49)

2 cups (480 ml) unsweetened nondairy milk (I like to use soy milk for this recipe)

2 tbsp (30 ml) fresh lemon juice

1 tbsp (15 ml) white wine vinegar

¼ tsp freshly ground black pepper

2 tsp (10 g) salt, divided, plus more to taste

Where are my garlic lovers? Gather round and get ready for this indulgent tangle of creamy, garlicky, restaurant-level fettuccine that you can make from scratch really easily. If you have never roasted garlic in its skin, quite frankly, you don't know what you are missing. It is absolutely deliciously mild and sweet, which is why we can get away with using two full heads in this recipe. If you aren't a garlic fan or don't have time to roast the garlic, there is no need to miss out on this slurpy, delicious pasta because it's still super delicious if you make it without!

Preheat the oven to 425°F (218°C) and brush a roughly 10-inch (25.5-cm) square piece of aluminum foil with the olive oil.

Cut the top quarter off each garlic head with a sharp knife so the cloves inside are exposed. Then place the largest parts, cut side down, in the middle of the foil. Draw the foil up around them, wrap and squeeze it tightly shut. Separately wrap the little pieces you cut off the top, too, and store in the fridge for another recipe.

Place the foil-wrapped garlic heads in the oven, directly on the oven shelf, and roast for about 40 minutes. Check whether they feel a little squishy through the foil. Return them to the oven for a few more minutes if not. If they are done, remove and set aside until cool enough to handle. The garlic can be roasted in this way up to 4 to 5 days before you make the alfredo and then stored in the fridge. I like to do it when I have the oven on to cook something else.

Make the sauce by opening the foil wrapping and squeezing the garlic cloves out of their silvery, papery skins from the root end, straight into your blender. They will pop out really easily. Add the cashews, almonds, nutritional yeast, nondairy milk, lemon juice, vinegar, pepper and 1 teaspoon of the salt; then blend until completely smooth. Taste to check the seasoning and add more salt, if necessary.

(continued)

1 lb (454 g) dried fettuccine or other pasta of choice

Bring a large pot of water to a rolling boil. Season with the remaining teaspoon of salt, add the fettuccine and cook for the time directed on the package. It usually takes around 8 minutes. When it's done, scoop out about ½ cup (120 ml) of the boiling water and set aside before draining the fettuccine. Return the fettuccine to the pot and immediately add the sauce. Return the pot to the stove and allow it to warm through over low heat for 3 to 4 minutes. It will thicken up a little as it warms up and you can loosen it to your liking with the starchy pasta water that you set aside. You won't need all of it; just add it a little at a time, if necessary. Serve as soon as the sauce has heated through.

Leftover sauce can be reheated. It will thicken up when refrigerated, but just loosen it up with a little nondairy milk, warm through and it will be good as new!

tips: *I like to top my Roasted Garlic Alfredo with some of my Cheesy Brazil Nut "Parm" (page 191) or some store-bought vegan cheese and red pepper flakes.*

I like to roast lots of garlic heads at once, squeeze out the soft garlic cloves and freeze them in ice cube trays so I always have roasted garlic on hand. It's great in recipes like this, spread on toast with some sea salt for a snack, spread in sandwiches or added to creamy sauces, mashed potato and hummus.

SWEET AND SMOKY GLAZED "MEATLOAF"

yield: 8 thick slices

1 tsp olive oil or water

1 small onion

4 cloves garlic

About 20 medium white or brown mushrooms (300 g)

2 cups (480 g) canned chickpeas, drained and rinsed, divided

¼ cup (28 g) ground flaxseeds

1 tsp salt

½ tsp freshly ground black pepper

½ cup (120 ml) BBQ sauce, divided, plus more for serving

1 tbsp (15 ml) pure maple syrup

2 tsp (10 ml) liquid smoke, or 2 tsp (4 g) smoked paprika

1 cup (80 g) rolled oats

Meatloaf has an almost iconic comfort food status and this vegan version is up there with the best of them. It's tender, has lots of texture and is totally delicious with its sweet and smoky flavors. You can use store-bought BBQ sauce or make the BBQ sauce from my Bangin' BBQ Cauliflower Wings (page 109). And if you don't have (or can't be bothered to make) BBQ sauce, tomato ketchup makes a great alternative, especially for children.

In a small sauté pan over medium heat, heat the oil or water. Sauté the onion for 5 to 6 minutes, or until golden, add the garlic and cook for a further 1 to 2 minutes. If using water to sauté, you will need to add more throughout the cooking process to prevent sticking. Turn off the heat and set aside.

Preheat the oven to 375°F (190°C) and line a 9 x 5–inch (23 x 12.5–cm) loaf pan with a strip of parchment paper lengthwise all the way down the middle, leaving some overhang on each side to act as handles to easily lift out the loaf.

Chop the mushrooms very finely. A food processor does this really quickly and easily. You might need to do it in batches. Once chopped, transfer to a large bowl.

Add 1 cup (240 g) of the chickpeas to the food processor along with the ground flaxseeds, salt, pepper, ¼ cup (60 ml) of the BBQ sauce, the maple syrup and liquid smoke. Process until smooth; then add the remaining cup (240 g) of chickpeas and the oats. Pulse a few times until the chickpeas are in smaller pieces and the oats have been broken down a little bit but are still quite chunky. Then use a spatula to scrape out the mixture into the bowl containing the mushrooms.

(continued)

SWEET AND SMOKY GLAZED "MEATLOAF" (CONTINUED)

½ cup (59 g) finely chopped walnuts (omit to make the recipe nut-free)

2 cups (216 g) dried vegan bread crumbs or panko

1 tsp dried thyme

1 tsp dried oregano

Add the sautéed onion and garlic, walnuts, bread crumbs, thyme and oregano to the bowl and, with clean hands, scrunch and mix it all together really well; then press down really tightly into the prepared pan. It will look as if there is too much, but once you have compacted it in there well, it will all fit.

Brush the top of the loaf with the remaining ¼ cup (60 ml) of BBQ sauce. Bake for 55 minutes to 1 hour on the middle shelf of the oven. Keep an eye on it toward the end and cover with some aluminum foil if the sauce on top starts to color too much. Once done, remove from the oven and allow to rest in the pan for at least 20 minutes before removing and slicing.

Leftovers will keep for up to 4 days in the fridge. Wrap in lightly greased aluminum foil and reheat in the oven. Slices are also pretty amazing when pan-fried until slightly crusty on each side. Cold, thin slices are great in sandwiches too!

tips: *The meatloaf can be prepared ahead of time, wrapped well in aluminum foil or plastic wrap and stored in the fridge for 2 to 3 days. Just add a few extra minutes to the cooking time when you bake it.*

When you have some stale bread, pop it into your food processor or blender to make bread crumbs, then freeze the crumbs in a sealed bag or container. They stay loose and don't freeze up into a solid lump and can be added straight into recipes like this one that call for bread crumbs.

HEAVENLY VEGGIE HOT POT

yield: 6 servings

1 tbsp (15 ml) olive oil or water, plus more oil for brushing (optional)

1 medium onion, finely chopped

2 celery ribs, finely chopped

4 cloves garlic, finely diced

¼ cup (60 g) tomato paste

2 slightly heaping cups (12 oz [350 g]) meatless crumbles/veggie ground round, or 2 cups (384 g) cooked green lentils

2 tsp (2 g) dried rosemary

2 tsp (1 g) dried mint or thyme

2 tbsp (16 g) all-purpose flour or cornstarch

2¼ cups (540 ml) vegetable or mushroom stock

¼ cup (60 ml) soy sauce or tamari (see note on page 62)

½ tsp liquid smoke (see note)

1½ tsp (8 g) salt, plus a pinch more for seasoning the top

½ tsp freshly ground black pepper

2 carrots, sliced into rounds

1 small (about 400 g) rutabaga, turnips or butternut squash, peeled and cut into ½" (1.3-cm) cubes

About 1 lb (454 g) potatoes

Olive oil cooking spray (optional)

My vegan twist on Lancashire hot pot. Simple, hearty, family-friendly comfort food! First, you sauce up some meatless crumbles or lentils in thick, rich, super-tasty gravy, and then you top it all with sliced raw potato and bake. The smell while it is cooking is unbelievably good, and the moment you pull it from the oven and see the gravy bubbling up around the golden brown potatoes will be a great one. Cozy fluffy sweaters or pajamas are optional, but a big appetite is mandatory.

In a large sauté pan, heat the oil or water (to prepare oil-free), over medium heat. Add the onion and celery and cook for about 6 minutes, or until the onion is translucent and just starting to turn golden. If using water, you will need to add a little more throughout the cooking process to prevent sticking.

Add the garlic and cook for a further minute. Then stir in the tomato paste, the meatless crumbles, rosemary, mint and flour. Add the stock gradually, about ½ cup (120 ml) at a time, working out any lumps in the mixture. Then add the soy sauce, liquid smoke, salt, pepper, carrots and rutabaga. Let it simmer away for 10 to 15 minutes. If using lentils, you might need to add a little more stock or water as it simmers if it starts to dry out too much, but it should be very thick and not liquid.

Meanwhile, preheat the oven to 400°F (200°C). Peel the potatoes and slice into rounds, as thinly as you can cut them (no more than ⅛ inch [3 mm] thick), producing enough slices to cover the surface area of a 2-quart (2-L)-capacity baking dish. The amount of potatoes you use will vary depending on how large or small the dish is. Do not place the potatoes in the dish yet.

Spoon the filling into the baking dish and top with the sliced potatoes, overlapping each one slightly. Brush or spray the potatoes with a little olive oil (omit to keep the recipe oil-free) and sprinkle with a pinch of salt. Bake for 50 to 60 minutes, or until the filling is bubbling up around the edges and the potatoes are soft and beginning to turn golden.

Leftovers will keep for 3 to 4 days in the fridge and reheat well.

note: *Liquid smoke is available in most grocery stores and is usually found near the condiments. A little goes a very long way, so be very careful not to add too much.*

SPICY CHILI WITH CORNBREAD CRUST

yield: 6 to 8 servings

chili

1 tbsp (15 ml) olive oil or water

1 medium onion, finely chopped

1 medium carrot, diced

1 celery rib, diced

4 cloves garlic, finely chopped

1 bell pepper, seeded and diced

24 oz (680 g) crushed tomatoes or passata

1 (15-oz [425-g]) can kidney beans, drained and rinsed

1 (15-oz [425-g]) can black beans, drained and rinsed

1 (15-oz [425-g]) can pinto beans, drained and rinsed

¾ cup (180 ml) vegetable stock or water

1 bay leaf

1 tbsp (12 g) cane or granulated white sugar

2 tbsp (16 g) chili powder (see note)

½ tsp red pepper flakes

½ tsp ground cumin

¼ tsp ground cinnamon

2 tsp (2 g) dried thyme

2 tsp (10 g) salt

¼ tsp freshly ground black pepper

1 tsp unsweetened cocoa powder, or 2 squares (about 0.2 oz [6 g]) good-quality dark chocolate

This, my friends, is an absolutely cozy-to-your-toes, comfort food winning combo. We're talking rich, flavor-packed chili, topped with golden cornbread batter, all baked up in the oven until crusty and bubbling. A little chocolate hit in the chili adds a really rich, earthy depth, so don't be tempted to skip it!

To prepare the chili, in a large skillet, heat the oil or water (for oil-free cooking) over medium heat. Add the onion, carrot and celery and sauté all together for 7 to 10 minutes, or until the onion is starting to turn golden. Then, add the garlic and bell pepper. If using water to sauté, you will need to add more throughout the cooking process as it evaporates. Cook for a further 2 minutes before adding all the other chili ingredients. Let the mixture come to a simmer; then allow it to gently bubble away for about 20 minutes. Remove the bay leaf and transfer to an 11 x 8 x 2½–inch (28 x 20.5 x 6.5–cm) casserole dish. If you use a casserole dish with a significantly larger surface area, you might not have enough cornbread batter to cover the top. Smooth out the chili to be level and preheat the oven to 375°F (190°C).

(continued)

cornbread

1 cup (130 g) cornmeal

1 cup (125 g) all-purpose flour or whole wheat flour, or 1½ cups (180 g) oat flour

¼ cup (50 g) cane or granulated white sugar

1 tbsp (12 g) baking powder

1 tsp salt

½ tsp ground cinnamon

1 tsp dried thyme

1 cup (240 ml) unsweetened soy milk

1 tbsp (15 ml) apple cider vinegar

¼ cup (60 ml) melted vegan butter or unsweetened applesauce (vegan butter gives the best flavor)

To prepare the cornbread batter, in a medium bowl, whisk together the cornmeal, flour, sugar, baking powder, salt, cinnamon and thyme. In another bowl, combine the soy milk and vinegar. Stir and allow to curdle for 1 minute; then add the melted vegan butter or applesauce and stir together. Pour this mixture into the dry ingredients and fold together. Do not overmix. Spoon the batter evenly over the top of the chili and spread it out so it mostly reaches the sides of the casserole. The layer of batter won't be very thick, so it's easier to dollop it out in spoonfuls all over and spread than it is to pour it all in one spot and then have to spread it out. A few tiny little gaps at the edges won't hurt and make it look really rustic when the chili bubbles up and over while cooking.

Bake for 30 to 35 minutes, or until the cornbread is cooked and the chili is bubbling nicely.

tip: The chili is lovely on its own minus the cornbread, too. Just let it cook on the stovetop for about 40 minutes, then serve. Try serving it on a bed of fluffy rice or on top of my Crispy Cornmeal Waffles (page 50).

note: In the United States, chili powder is a blend of chile pepper and other herbs and spices. It is very different than European-style chili powder, which tends to contain just chile pepper and is much hotter. If you don't have access to American-style, just use ½ to 1 teaspoon of European-style chili powder instead of the 2 tablespoons (16 g) listed here.

NEXT-LEVEL MUSHROOM LASAGNA

yield: 8 servings

béchamel sauce

2 tbsp (30 ml) olive oil or vegan butter (optional)

½ cup (63 g) all-purpose flour

2¾ cups (660 ml) unsweetened nondairy milk

¼ cup (28 g) nutritional yeast (see note on page 49)

1 tbsp (16 g) white miso paste (see note on page 84)

Pinch of ground nutmeg

Salt and freshly ground black pepper

lasagna

1½ lb (680 g) white, cremini or portobello mushrooms

2 tbsp (30 ml) olive oil or water, divided

3 cloves garlic, finely chopped

¼ tsp salt, or to taste

¼ tsp freshly ground black pepper, or to taste

Layer upon layer of tangy, rich marinara sauce, creamy béchamel, garlicky mushrooms and deep green spinach, all held together by blankets of thick, soft lasagna noodles. This is next-level comfort food and like a big warm hug, it will keep you coming back for more. To make things easier, you can prep the individual components a day or two ahead, and although it's better if you make your own marinara sauce, it' also perfectly acceptable to use store-bought, so do whatever works for you. Either way, you will have yourself a cozy pan of creamy, saucy, totally delicious lasagna!

To prepare the béchamel, in a small saucepan, heat the olive oil over medium heat. Add the flour. Stir really well to combine and cook for 1 to 2 minutes, stirring constantly. This will remove the raw flour taste and it will start smelling a little nutty. Gradually add the nondairy milk, ½ cup (120 ml) at a time, whisking constantly to work out the lumps. Alternatively, if you prefer oil-free cooking, skip this step and instead, in a small saucepan, simply stir the milk into the flour very gradually to work out any lumps; then place over medium heat and continue as directed. Keep whisking for 5 to 8 minutes, or until the sauce thickens. It should be thick enough to coat the back of a wooden spoon. If it gets too thick, add an extra drop of milk to loosen it a little. Then add the nutritional yeast, miso paste and nutmeg and stir for another minute or two, until the miso melts in and is incorporated. Season to taste with salt and pepper; then remove from the heat and set aside.

Prepare the lasagna. Wipe any dirt from the mushrooms, and dice into roughly ¼-inch (6-mm) square pieces.

In a large skillet, heat 1 tablespoon (15 ml) of the olive oil (or water, if cooking oil-free) over medium heat, and then add the mushrooms, garlic, salt and pepper. Keep them moving and cook until the mushrooms release their liquid, and it evaporates again, 10 to 15 minutes. If you don't have a large skillet, you may need to do this in 2 batches. Remove from the heat and set aside.

(continued)

lasagna (cont.)

11 oz (315 g) dried lasagna sheets (about 15)

3 cups (720 ml) Marinara Sauce (page 67) or a good-quality store-bought, divided

3 cups (90 g) spinach, well rinsed

¾ to 1 cup (90 to 120 g) Cheesy Brazil Nut "Parm" (page 191), or 1 cup (112 g) grated vegan cheese

Precook the lasagna sheets in a large pan of boiling water to which you have added the remaining tablespoon (15 ml) of olive oil (skip the oil for oil-free cooking) until they are al dente. This usually takes about 8 minutes. If the lasagna sheet label says "no precook," soak them in a single layer in boiling water for 5 minutes. Drain and lay them out on a clean dish towel or some baking parchment until you need them.

Preheat the oven to 350°F (175°C). Then, in a 9 x 13–inch (23 x 33–cm) baking dish, smear about ¾ cup (180 ml) of the marinara sauce and about ¼ cup (60 ml) of the béchamel over the bottom. Swirl them up together, and then top with enough lasagna sheets to cover the entire dish, trimming them, if necessary, to make them fit with as few gaps as possible.

Top with a layer of béchamel (about ⅓ cup [80 ml] should be sufficient), a layer of marinara (about ¾ cup [180 ml]), half of the mushrooms, followed by half of the spinach leaves spread out evenly. Top with more lasagna sheets and repeat the layers as before, topping with a final layer of lasagna sheets. Spread with the remainder of the marinara, and all of the remaining béchamel. Swirl them together. Finally, sprinkle with a generous amount of Cheesy Brazil Nut "Parm" or vegan cheese.

Bake, uncovered, for 35 to 40 minutes, or until bubbling and golden. Remove from the oven and let rest for 10 minutes before serving.

tip: *Once assembled and before baking, the lasagna can be covered and refrigerated for up to 3 days, and then cooked as directed. It can also be baked, and cooled and refrigerated for up to 3 days, and then reheated. If previously baked, wrap it in foil prior to reheating to prevent the top from getting too dark.*

THE BEST BAKED MAC AND "CHEESE"

yield: 4 or 5 servings

3 slices vegan bread (slightly stale is best)

3 tbsp (45 g) vegan butter, divided, or 2 tbsp (30 ml) olive oil (both are optional)

1 clove garlic

2 cups (266 g) peeled and diced sweet potato (½" [1.3-cm] cubes)

¼ small cauliflower (about 9 oz [255 g]), broken into florets

5 tbsp (90 g) white miso paste or chickpea miso paste (see note)

1¾ tsp (9 g) salt

¾ cup (84 g) nutritional yeast (see note on page 49)

1 tsp prepared yellow mustard

1 tbsp (8 g) arrowroot powder or cornstarch

1 cup (240 ml) unsweetened nondairy milk

1 tbsp (15 ml) white wine vinegar (gives the best cheesy flavor, but apple cider vinegar could also be used)

¼ tsp onion powder

¼ tsp garlic powder

⅛ tsp smoked paprika or chipotle powder

14 oz (400 g) dried macaroni pasta

Nothing is heavier on those comfort food vibes than a saucy, cheesy, crispy-topped mac and cheese. And, yes, I know that a good vegan mac and cheese is hard to come by, but this one really does check all the right boxes. For me, mac and cheese should always have a crispy top, and this one doesn't disappoint. The irresistible, golden, buttery, garlicky bread crumb sprinkles tip it right over the edge and make it comforting on every level. This is where it's at, friends!

Break up the slices of bread into smaller pieces and place them in a blender or food processor with 2 tablespoons (30 g) of the vegan butter or olive oil and the garlic. Pulse until reduced to fine bread crumbs. Transfer to a bowl and set aside. To keep oil-free, omit the butter or oil.

In a saucepan, combine the sweet potato and cauliflower and cover with water. Bring to a boil and simmer for 10 to 15 minutes, or until fork-tender. Drain and transfer to a blender. Add the miso, salt, nutritional yeast, mustard, arrowroot powder, nondairy milk, vinegar, onion powder, garlic powder, smoked paprika and the remaining tablespoon (15 g) of vegan butter to the blender, and blend until completely smooth. Again, omit the butter if you want to keep it oil-free.

Bring a large saucepan of water to a boil. Then add the macaroni and cook just until tender using the timing on the package directions as a guide.

Meanwhile, preheat the oven to 400°F (200°C).

Drain the pasta, return it to the pot and add the sauce, stirring to combine. Spoon the mac and cheese into a baking dish and sprinkle the bread crumb mixture evenly over the top. Bake for 20 to 25 minutes, or until golden and crisp. For extra crispness, you can broil it for a few minutes at the end, if you like, but keep a careful eye on it, as, like toast, it will go from golden to burnt in a matter of seconds.

Serve immediately.

note: *Miso can be purchased in most grocery stores and is usually found in a container in the refrigerator case. Be careful when buying it because it comes in all sorts of varieties. For this recipe, you need white miso, sometimes labeled "sweet white miso" (note that it isn't actually white but more of a creamy beige color). Don't use the darker red or brown varieties. Because miso is fermented, leftovers will keep in the fridge for a very long time.*

STICKY SWEET-AND-SOUR TOFU

yield: 3 or 4 servings

1 large block (about 12 oz [350 g]) extra-firm tofu

2 tbsp (16 g) all-purpose flour or cornstarch

1 tsp Chinese five-spice powder

½ tsp salt, divided

2 tbsp (30 ml) tamari, soy sauce or coconut aminos, divided

2 tbsp (30 ml) sesame oil or other oil of choice, divided

1 tbsp (8 g) arrowroot powder or cornstarch

½ cup (120 ml) pineapple juice (from the can if you are using canned pineapple, below, or freshly juiced if you are using fresh)

⅓ cup (80 g) tomato ketchup

2 tbsp (30 ml) sriracha (optional; you can use more ketchup instead)

¼ cup (50 g) cane or granulated white sugar

¼ cup (60 ml) rice vinegar or apple cider vinegar

Pinch of freshly ground black or white pepper

1 small onion, sliced into half-moons

2 bell peppers (different colors), seeded and thinly sliced

3 cloves garlic, finely chopped

1 heaping cup (165 g) fresh or canned pineapple chunks

Skip the takeout and make this recipe instead! It's fruity, it's sharp and it's sweet, but not tooth-achingly so, like some you might have had in the past. Served over fluffy rice, it's comfort food to the max, but healthy, light and fun at the same time. Oh, and do you want to know a really great tofu tip? When you buy it, toss it into the freezer in its packaging; then defrost before you need it, press it thoroughly to remove the liquid, and then continue on with this or any other similar tofu recipe. It really improves the texture!

Open the tofu package, drain the water, then either press in a tofu press or wrap it in paper towels or a clean dish towel and put something heavy on top. I usually use a heavy cutting board and some cookbooks. Let it sit like this for 15 minutes, unwrap and cut it into ½-inch (1.3-cm) cubes.

While the tofu is pressing, preheat the oven to 400°F (200°C). Line a baking sheet with parchment paper.

In a bowl large enough to hold the tofu, stir together the flour, Chinese five-spice powder, just ¼ teaspoon of the salt, 1 tablespoon (15 ml) of the tamari and 1 tablespoon (15 ml) of the oil to form a paste. Toss the tofu cubes in the paste until they are all coated. If you have trouble coating them, use your fingers to rub the paste over the tofu pieces. Spread out on the prepared baking sheet and bake, tossing once at the 15-minute point, for 25 to 30 minutes, or until really golden.

While the tofu is cooking, place the arrowroot powder in a small bowl and gradually add the pineapple juice, stirring constantly to work out any lumps. Stir in the ketchup, sriracha (if using) sugar, vinegar, the remaining tablespoon (15 ml) of tamari, remaining ¼ teaspoon of salt and the pepper. Set this pineapple sauce aside.

About 5 minutes before the tofu is ready, or just after it comes out of the oven, in a large skillet or wok, heat the remaining tablespoon (15 ml) of oil over medium-high heat, and stir-fry the onion and bell peppers for 3 to 4 minutes; then add the garlic and cook for another minute. Pour in the pineapple sauce and keep stirring everything around until the sugar crystals have dissolved and the sauce has thickened. Lower the heat to low and add the tofu cubes and pineapple chunks. Allow to warm through, and then serve over fluffy rice or some noodles.

AWESOMELY EASY CRISPY POTATO TACOS

yield: 6 to 8 tacos

1 lb (454 g) potatoes, peeled and cut into ½" (1.3-cm) cubes

¼ cup (60 g) tomato paste

1 tbsp (15 ml) sriracha or other hot chili sauce

2 tsp (6 g) garlic powder

2 tsp (5 g) onion powder

¼ cup (30 g) cornmeal or semolina

1 tsp salt

2 tbsp (30 ml) olive oil or water

to assemble

8 corn tortillas

Guacamole

Toppings of choice (I like to use lettuce, halved cherry tomatoes, jalapeño peppers, fresh cilantro and salsa)

Colorful, crispy, slightly spicy potatoes all baked up and tucked inside toasty, warm corn tortillas with all the toppings . . . what's not to love?

Preheat the oven to 425°F (218°C). Line a baking sheet with parchment paper.

Place the potatoes in a bowl.

In another small bowl, combine the tomato paste, sriracha, garlic powder, onion powder, cornmeal, salt and olive oil or water (for oil-free cooking) and mix well together. Spoon the mixture over the potatoes and toss really well to coat; then spread them out on the prepared baking sheet. Make sure they are in a single layer and leave a little space around each cube.

Bake for 25 minutes, remove from the oven, turn over, and bake again for another 20 to 25 minutes, or until really crispy and turning golden.

Assemble the tacos. Heat the tortillas in batches in a skillet over medium heat, flipping to warm each side, and then stack them on a plate covered with a clean dish towel to keep warm.

Spread each tortilla with guacamole. Top with crispy potatoes and your other toppings of choice.

tip: *These crispy potatoes are not just good on tacos. Cook them on their own and serve as a side with other meals, too.*

SUPER CREAMY BUTTERNUT SQUASH AND SAGE RISOTTO

yield: 3 or 4 servings

1 medium butternut squash (about 3 lb [1.4 kg])

2 tbsp (30 ml) olive oil, divided

½ cup (70 g) raw cashews (soaked in boiling water for at least 15 minutes, then drained, unless you have a high-powered blender)

2 tbsp (14 g) nutritional yeast (see note on page 49)

½ cup (120 ml) water

1 medium onion, finely chopped

5 cloves garlic, finely chopped

1 cup (200 g) short-grain risotto rice (Carnaroli, Arborio or Vialone Nano)

1 cup (240 ml) white wine

This is one of my favorite dinners when I really want to relax and treat myself. It's comforting on so many levels. There is a lot of stirring involved, but I recommend doing that with a glass of wine in hand. It makes it infinitely more enjoyable and turns the whole process into an almost therapeutic experience. Escape to the kitchen, throw on some tunes and spend a mindless, relaxing 20 minutes watching a pile of dried rice transform into a creamy, delicious mass before your very eyes. Traditional risottos are finished with lots of Parmesan and butter to make them super creamy and luxurious. To re-create that in a vegan-friendly way, I like to make a rich cashew cream, which gets stirred through at the end to produce that "wallowing in luxury" kind of texture all good risottos should have.

Preheat the oven to 400°F (200°C). Line a baking sheet with parchment paper.

Peel the butternut squash and cut in half. Scoop out and discard the seeds. Cut the squash into ½-inch (1.3-cm) cubes. Toss with 1 tablespoon (15 ml) of the olive oil, spread out in a single layer on the prepared baking sheet and bake for 30 to 40 minutes, or until tender and the edges of the cubes are just starting to turn golden.

Meanwhile, prepare the cashew cream. In a blender, combine the cashews, nutritional yeast and water and blend until completely smooth. Set aside.

In a large sauté pan, heat the remaining tablespoon (15 ml) of olive oil over medium heat and add the onion. Sauté for about 10 minutes, or until golden; then add the garlic and rice. Stir constantly for a couple of minutes to toast the rice. Then add the wine and keep stirring until it has almost completely absorbed.

(continued)

2 cups (480 ml) flavorful vegetable stock

2 tsp (2 g) chopped fresh sage

2 tbsp (30 g) vegan butter

Salt and freshly ground black pepper

to serve

Cheezy Brazil Nut "Parm" (page 191), or store bought vegan Parmesan

Preheat the oven to 400°F (200°C).

Add the stock ½ cup (120 ml) at a time, stirring constantly between each addition and only adding more once the previous stock has been absorbed. By the time you have used all of the stock, the rice should be tender. This will take 15 to 20 minutes.

By now, the squash should be cooked. Lower the heat under the risotto to low and add half of the squash pieces. Gently mash them with a fork or spatula and stir them well into the rice. Then add the rest of the squash pieces, leaving them whole, along with the cashew cream, sage and vegan butter; then stir really well. Add salt and pepper to taste and allow the risotto to heat through for 3 to 4 minutes before serving.

Serve the risotto with my Cheezy Brazil Nut "Parm" or store-bought vegan Parmesan.

Leftovers will keep for a few days and reheat well. Add a drop of water while reheating to loosen it up a little.

tips: *Do not rinse the rice when making risotto. The starch is what makes it really creamy, and if you rinse first, you will wash it all away.*

If you want to impress, make some crispy sage leaves as a garnish. In a small skillet, heat 3 tablespoons (45 ml) of olive oil over medium heat and drop in a few fresh sage leaves. Watch them carefully but don't touch them. They will start to turn darker. Once they have become dark green all over, they should feel almost crisp. Gently remove them with a spatula and transfer them to a paper towel. As they cool, they will crisp up even more. Be very gentle with them as they are brittle and break very easily.

SHEPHERDLESS PIE WITH ROOT VEG MASH

yield: 5 or 6 servings

1 medium rutabaga, peeled and chopped into 1" (2.5-cm) chunks

1 medium parsnip, peeled and chopped into 1" (2.5-cm) chunks

4 medium carrots, peeled and chopped into 1" (2.5-cm) chunks

2 large potatoes, peeled and chopped into 1" (2.5-cm) chunks

1 tsp salt, plus more to taste

1 tbsp (15 g) vegan butter (optional)

Up to ⅓ cup (80 ml) unsweetened nondairy milk

Freshly ground black pepper

2 tsp (10 ml) olive oil or water

1 medium onion, chopped finely

4 cloves garlic, chopped finely

1 cup (192 g) dried green lentils

2½ cups (600 ml) vegetable stock, divided

1 cup (240 ml) water

1 bay leaf

As I'm British, a potato queen (I love them so much!) and a lover of all things gravy, it would be criminal of me not to include my take on shepherd's pie. It's the kind of food that brings a smile to everyone's face when it's presented in all its bubbling, golden glory at the table. The perfect shepherd's pie should be full of robust, hearty ingredients with rich, savory gravy and a blanket of smooth mash. Using a combination of root veg and potatoes keeps it creamy and adds a lovely gentle sweetness, but if you don't have any root veggies on hand, or want to keep the recipe more budget-friendly, just use all potatoes. About eight to nine medium ones should suffice.

In a large saucepan, combine the rutabaga, parsnip, carrots and potatoes. Add the salt, cover with water, bring to a boil and cook for around 25 minutes, or until they are tender enough to mash. Drain the vegetables, return them to the pan and allow them to steam dry for a few minutes. Add the vegan butter (if using) and mash really well. Add the nondairy milk as needed to help make mashing easier and for additional creaminess. You might not need all of it. Add salt and pepper to taste; then set aside.

Meanwhile, in a large skillet, heat the oil or water (for oil-free cooking) over medium heat. Add the onion and cook for 3 to 4 minutes. Then add the garlic and cook for 1 minute more. If using water to sauté, add a little more throughout the cooking process to prevent sticking. Pour in the lentils, cover with 2 cups (480 ml) of the vegetable stock and the cup (240 ml) of water, add the bay leaf, bring to a simmer and lower the heat to medium-low. Cook until the lentils are tender but not mushy, 25 to 30 minutes.

While they are cooking, preheat the oven to 400°F (200°C).

(continued)

2 tbsp (16 g) arrowroot powder or cornstarch

2½ tsp (6 g) dried mixed herbs or a combination of thyme, rosemary and marjoram

3 tbsp (45 ml) soy sauce or tamari (see note on page 62)

1 cup (240 g) crushed canned tomatoes or passata

1 cup (134 g) frozen peas

10 white, cremini or baby bella mushrooms, diced

Vegan butter or olive oil, for baking (optional)

After 25 to 30 minutes, most of the liquid should be absorbed by the lentils. Remove the bay leaf. Then add the arrowroot powder and dried herbs and stir really well before adding the soy sauce, crushed tomatoes, the remaining ½ cup (120 ml) of stock, the peas and mushrooms. Stir together and add salt and pepper to taste. It will be really thick. Transfer to a casserole dish, and top with the mashed vegetables. Spread the mash out evenly and rough up the top with a fork.

Place on a baking sheet. You can dot the top with vegan butter or drizzle it with olive oil to make it extra crispy, if you like, but it isn't necessary. Bake, uncovered, for 30 to 40 minutes, or until bubbling well around the edges. You can finish it off under the broiler for a few minutes if you want to brown the top more.

Leftovers will keep in the fridge for 3 to 4 days and reheat really well.

tip: *The pie can be frozen once assembled and before baking. Be sure it is completely cool and cover well. Thaw when needed and bake as directed.*

THE WHOLE ENCHILADA CASSEROLE

yield: 6 servings

1 recipe Mind-Blowing Jalapeño Queso (page 117), made as described but without heating it after blending

28 oz (793 g) fire-roasted or regular diced or crushed tomatoes

1 medium onion, halved, divided

3 cloves garlic, finely chopped

1 tsp salt

2 tbsp (16 g) chili powder (see note on page 80)

1 tsp ground cumin

1 tsp dried oregano

3 tbsp (45 ml) pure maple syrup

1 tbsp (15 ml) oil of choice

2 bell peppers (different colors), seeded and diced

1 (15-oz [425-g]) can black beans, drained and rinsed

1 (15-oz [425-g]) can pinto beans, drained and rinsed

1 (4.5-oz [127-g]) can chopped green chiles, undrained

2 cups (328 g) frozen corn kernels

12 (7" to 8" [18- to 20.5-cm]) corn tortillas, cut in half

1 cup (112 g) shredded vegan cheese

All the warm, comforting flavors of enchiladas, layered up with jalapeño queso, topped with vegan cheese and baked until golden and bubbling. We're talking tangy, spicy, smoky, cheesy, not super authentic but ultra delicious! This casserole takes a little time and involves a few steps—but it's all super easy—such as turning on the oven, pressing a button on the blender and assembling your tasty, lasagna-esque layers like a boss. You can even make the queso, the enchilada sauce and the filling up to three days in advance. Then put it all together at a later date or assemble the whole thing, cover tightly and pop it in the fridge or freezer for another day.

Pour the jalapeño queso into a bowl and set aside. You can do this up to 3 to 4 days ahead of time and keep refrigerated until needed.

Make the enchilada sauce. In a blender, combine the fire-roasted tomatoes, half of the onion, garlic, salt, chili powder, cumin, oregano and maple syrup. Blend until smooth. This, too, can be done up to 3 to 4 days ahead.

Chop the remaining onion half. In a large sauté pan, heat the oil over medium heat and sauté the onion for about 5 minutes until transparent. Add the bell peppers and cook for another 5 minutes, stirring frequently.

Add the enchilada sauce to the pan along with the drained beans, green chiles (including any liquid) and frozen corn. Once the mixture is just starting to bubble and the corn kernels have defrosted, remove from the heat.

Meanwhile, preheat the oven to 375°F (190°C) and have ready a 9 x 13–inch (23 x 33–cm) casserole.

Pour about 1 cup (240 ml) of the queso into the bottom of the casserole and spread it out evenly. Top with 4 halved tortillas and cover them with about one-third of the bean mixture. Spread about one-third of the remaining queso over the beans, and then top with another 4 halved tortillas. Repeat with more beans, half of the remaining queso, another layer of tortillas, the remaining beans and remaining queso.

Sprinkle with the shredded vegan cheese and bake for 30 minutes. Remove from the oven and let sit for 10 minutes before serving.

Leftovers will keep for up to 4 days in the fridge and reheat really well.

SMOKY TOMATO AND WHITE BEAN SOUP

yield: 4 or 5 servings

1 tbsp (15 ml) olive oil or water

1 large onion, finely chopped

2 celery ribs, finely chopped

5 cloves garlic, finely chopped

1 tsp smoked paprika or chipotle powder

½ tsp ground cumin

¼ cup (60 g) tomato paste

27 oz (765 g) canned chopped fire-roasted tomatoes

2 tsp (10 g) salt, plus more to taste

½ tsp freshly ground black pepper

3 cups (720 ml) vegetable stock

1 tbsp (12 g) cane or granulated white sugar

4½ cups (1.2 kg) white kidney, cannellini or lima beans, drained and rinsed

Serve this brimming-with-flavor soup in deep bowls that you can cozily wrap your hands around on a chilly evening. It's easy to make, easy to eat and one of those recipes that gets even more flavorful with time, so it is perfect for making ahead. It even freezes well. My No-Knead Focaccia (page 121) is its perfect partner.

In a large skillet, heat the olive oil or water (for oil-free cooking) over medium heat. Sauté the onion and celery for about 10 minutes, until they are starting to go golden brown. If you are using water to sauté, you will need to add a little more water every few minutes to prevent the onion and celery from sticking.

Add the garlic, smoked paprika and cumin and continue to cook for another 2 minutes, stirring constantly. Then add all the other ingredients. Stir well to combine, allow to come to a simmer and cook for another 20 minutes. Add a little water to adjust the consistency to your liking, check the seasoning and adjust to taste; then serve. I like the soup chunky, but you can use an immersion blender right in the pan to make it smoother and creamier, if you want to.

tips: *Make this soup with only 1½ to 2 cups (360 to 480 ml) of stock instead of 3 cups (720 ml), so it's more like a thick stew, and serve it over rice, quinoa or couscous.*

FEEL-GOOD POTATO AND CHICKPEA CURRY

yield: 6 servings

1 large onion, divided

1 celery rib, cut into chunks

5 cloves garlic

1 jalapeño pepper, left whole with the stem removed

1 tbsp (15 ml) oil or water

3 tbsp (26 g) curry powder

½ tsp ground cinnamon

2 cups (480 g) canned crushed tomatoes or passata

¾ cup (180 ml) water

2 large potatoes (about 21 oz [600 g] total), peeled and cut into ½" (1.3-cm) cubes

2 lemongrass stalks (optional)

½ cup (75 g) frozen peas

3 cups (720 g) chickpeas, drained and rinsed

1 (13.5-oz [382-ml]) can light or full-fat coconut milk

1 tsp salt, plus more to taste

Satisfy all your spicy comfort food cravings with this easy and super-flavorful curry. It's wrapped-in-a-sweater, comforting, cozy food at its best and it is completely necessary to serve this over a giant pile of steaming rice with a big dollop of mango chutney and a fluffy naan on the side!

Peel and cut the onion in half. Cut one half into thin half-moon slices and set aside. Cut the other half in two and place in a food processor along with the celery, garlic and stemmed jalapeño. Process for 1 to 2 minutes, or until a smooth paste is formed.

In a large skillet, heat the oil or water (for oil-free cooking) over medium heat. Add the sliced onion and sauté for 3 to 4 minutes, or until translucent. If using water to sauté, you will need to add a little more occasionally to prevent sticking. Sprinkle in the curry powder and cinnamon and cook, stirring, for a further 1 to 2 minutes, until the mixture smells fragrant; then add the onion paste. Cook for 10 minutes, stirring frequently.

Add the crushed tomatoes, water and potato cubes. Split the lemongrass stalks lengthwise with a sharp knife prior to adding, and hit it really hard along the length with a rolling pin or the bottom of a heavy pan. This will help maximize the flavor. Add them to the skillet, give it all a good stir and allow to simmer for 15 to 20 minutes, or until the potatoes are fork-tender.

Add the frozen peas and chickpeas, the coconut milk and salt, stir, and then simmer for another 15 minutes, or until heated through and bubbling. You can serve now, or lower the heat to really low and leave to simmer for up to an hour. Be sure to remove and discard the lemongrass before serving.

tip: *If you prefer a hotter curry, add ½ to 1 teaspoon of crushed red pepper flakes in addition to the jalapeño, or swap out the jalapeño for a fierier chile pepper instead.*

CAULI-POWER BURGERS

yield: 8 burgers

2 tsp (10 ml) olive oil or water

1 medium onion, finely chopped

½ medium cauliflower, broken into florets (about 4 heaping cups [400 g])

6 oz (170 g) medium, firm or extra-firm tofu (no need to press it)

3 cloves garlic

3 tbsp (45 g) cashew or almond butter

2 tbsp (16 g) arrowroot powder or cornstarch

½ cup (60 g) cornmeal

3 tbsp (21 g) ground flaxseeds

½ tsp ground cumin

1 tsp salt

¼ tsp freshly ground black pepper

½ tsp ground turmeric

1 tsp chipotle powder or smoked paprika

¼ cup (28 g) nutritional yeast (see note on page 49)

1 tsp dried oregano

1 cup (80 g) rolled oats

Soft, mushy vegan burgers that fall apart or squirt out the other side when you bite into them are a pet peeve of mine. These are none of that. They are firm, chewy and hearty. Want to know my trick for making veggie burgers that don't fall apart? Nut butter! It acts like glue and holds them together perfectly. Once baked, these burgers get a lovely crusty, golden brown exterior that is just screaming to be doused in sauces, loaded with toppings and packed into a soft bun. Try them with my Easy Garlic Ranch Dressing (page 201) or Avocado Crema (page 126). A big, fat, crispy onion ring squeezed in there somewhere is highly recommended, too!

In a small sauté pan, heat the oil or water (for oil-free cooking) over medium heat; then, add the onion and sauté for 8 to 10 minutes, or until golden. If using water to sauté, you will need to add a little more throughout the cooking process to prevent sticking. Remove from the heat and set aside to cool.

Preheat the oven to 400°F (200°C) and line a large baking sheet with parchment paper.

Place the cauliflower in a food processor. Pulse until the cauliflower looks a bit like rice. Remove the blade and spoon the riced cauliflower into a large bowl.

Put the food processor back together (no need to wash it); then add the tofu, garlic, cashew butter, arrowroot powder, cornmeal, flaxseeds, cumin, salt, pepper, turmeric, chipotle powder, nutritional yeast and oregano. Process on full speed until a completely smooth paste is formed and it starts to ball up. Then, add the oats and run the food processor for about 10 seconds, or until they are a little bit broken up but still chunky and incorporated into the paste.

Add the cooled sautéed onion to the riced cauliflower. Stir together and add the tofu mixture. Using clean hands, get in there and scrunch and knead everything together really well.

Using about a tennis ball–size quantity per burger (make them smaller if you prefer), shape into patties ½ to ¾ inch (1.3 to 2 cm) thick and lay them out on the prepared baking sheet. Bake for 15 minutes; then flip them over carefully and cook for another 10 to 15 minutes or until a nice crust has developed on the outside.

the munchies

Here follows a whole chapter of delicious munchies designed for you to share with a crowd or to snaffle at home by yourself. I might have done that with the Pizza Party Pull-Apart Bread (113). Ssshhh . . . don't tell anyone!

These appetizers and snacks set the stage for the whole feast, or can be the feast themselves. With everything from my take on classic spinach and artichoke dip (page 106), to sharing bread (page 113) and the best potato salad (page 110) you have ever eaten in your life, there is something for every occasion.

My husband and I often have what we call a "pick it night" when we have lots of different appies to eat with some beer or wine, rather than a big dinner. I hope you can enjoy plenty of your own "pick it nights" with some of these. They make stuffing your face with copious amounts of snack food feel altogether more acceptable.

SHOWSTOPPING BAKED SPINACH AND ARTICHOKE DIP

yield: 8 to 10 servings

1 tbsp (15 ml) olive oil or water

1 medium onion, finely chopped

4 cloves garlic, finely chopped

12 oz (350 g) silken tofu

½ cup (120 ml) unsweetened nondairy milk (I think soy milk gives the best flavor)

3 tbsp (24 g) tapioca starch, arrowroot powder or cornstarch (tapioca starch gives best results)

1 tsp salt

¼ tsp freshly ground black pepper

⅓ cup (37 g) nutritional yeast (see note on page 49)

1 tbsp (15 ml) white wine vinegar

8 oz (227 g) vegan cream cheese

2 packed cups (60 g) spinach leaves, well rinsed

1 (14-oz [400-g]) can artichoke hearts in brine

½ to 1 cup (60 to 120 g) Cheesy Brazil Nut "Parm" (page 191) or vegan mozzarella cheese shreds (optional)

Nothing says the party's here like a big dish of warm spinach and artichoke dip! It's the perfect crave-worthy appetizer. It's soft and creamy with loads of flavor and is great eaten warm or at room temperature. Serve it with chips, crackers, baguette slices, vegetable sticks, raw radishes (weird, I know, but it works!), toast or even garlic bread (page 125). I recommend using canned artichokes in brine over the ones you can buy in oil, for the tang they give. It helps cut through the creaminess and adds more depth to the flavor.

In a small skillet, heat the olive oil or water over medium heat. Add the onion and sauté for 10 to 15 minutes, or until caramelized and golden. If you use water, you will need to add a little more gradually throughout, to prevent the onion from sticking. Add the chopped garlic in the last 2 minutes of cooking; then remove the pan from the heat and set aside. Preheat the oven to 400°F (200°C).

In a blender, combine the silken tofu, nondairy milk, tapioca starch, salt, pepper, nutritional yeast, vinegar and vegan cream cheese and blend until smooth.

Shred the spinach leaves. Drain the artichokes and chop roughly into small, chunky pieces. Combine the spinach and artichoke in a large bowl, add the onion mixture and pour the tofu mixture over them. Stir really well and pour into a baking dish or ovenproof skillet. Top with a sprinkle of the Parm (if using) and bake for 30 minutes, or until starting to turn golden on top and bubbly around the edges.

Leftovers can be reheated gently in the oven or microwave, or can be enjoyed cold.

tip: Prep up to a day ahead; then cover and store in the fridge overnight. Just add 5 minutes to the baking time.

BANGIN' BBQ CAULIFLOWER WINGS

yield: 4 or 5 servings

cauliflower

1 tsp oil of choice, for pan

¾ cup (94 g) all-purpose flour

¼ cup (30 g) cornmeal (good for texture, or use more all-purpose flour, if you like)

1 tsp salt

1 tsp onion powder

1 tsp garlic powder

½ tsp dried thyme

½ tsp freshly ground black pepper

½ cup (120 ml) unsweetened nondairy milk

½ cup (120 ml) water

1 medium cauliflower, broken into bite-size florets

BBQ sauce

½ to 1 jalapeño pepper, left whole with just the stalk removed, or halved if you want less kick

13 oz (370 g) tomato paste

1 cup (240 ml) pineapple juice (from a can, carton or freshly squeezed)

⅓ cup (70 g) dark brown sugar or coconut sugar

¼ cup (60 ml) blackstrap molasses

⅓ cup + 2 tbsp (110 ml) apple cider vinegar

1 tsp garlic powder

1 tsp onion powder

1 tsp liquid smoke (see note on page 76)

Finger-lickin' comfort food to rock your world! These tender wings are first baked in their batter coating, and then brushed in BBQ sauce before being rebaked to get those flavors all soaked in. They are saucy, sticky, spicy, fruity, sweet and very addictive. Serve them up with my creamy, garlicky ranch dressing (page 201) for dipping and you've got the best combo ever. They are perfect as an appetizer but are also great as part of a meal. We love them tumbled on top of a big, crispy salad with the ranch used as the salad dressing, but you could also serve them atop Buddha bowls. Make plenty because once you start eating them, you just can't stop!

1 tsp salt

1 tsp prepared yellow mustard

½ tsp freshly ground black pepper

Preheat the oven to 425°F (218°C) and line a large baking sheet with parchment paper. Grease the parchment with a light brush of any cooking oil.

In a bowl, whisk together the flour, cornmeal, salt, onion powder, garlic powder, thyme and black pepper. Gradually add the nondairy milk and water, whisking as you go, to work out the lumps and create a smooth batter.

Add the cauliflower florets to the batter and stir to coat evenly. Remove the florets and let any excess batter drip off. Then lay them on the prepared baking sheet, leaving a little space around each one. Bake for 25 minutes.

Meanwhile, prepare the BBQ sauce. In a blender, combine all the ingredients and blend until completely smooth.

Remove the cauliflower from the oven and brush really generously in the BBQ sauce, making sure to cover all sides. Return the cauliflower to the oven and bake for another 15 to 30 minutes, or longer, until the florets are at your desired stickiness. The longer you bake them, the stickier they get.

tip: *Leftover BBQ sauce will keep for up to 1 week in the fridge and freezes well.*

KICKED-UP CREAMY TANGY POTATO SALAD

yield: 6 to 8 servings

2 tbsp (30 ml) white wine vinegar

1 tbsp (16 g) Dijon mustard

2 cloves garlic, very finely chopped

¼ cup (60 g) unsweetened applesauce

1 tbsp (15 ml) pure maple syrup or (12 g) cane or granulated white sugar

2 tbsp (30 ml) water

2⅛ tsp (11 g) salt, divided

⅛ tsp freshly ground black pepper

2 lb (1 kg) potatoes, peeled and cut into ½" (1.3-cm) cubes

7 oz (198 g) bacon-style tempeh strips, smoked tempeh or any other vegan bacon product

Oil, for griddle or skillet (optional)

¾ to 1 cup (180 to 240 ml) vegan mayonnaise

2 tbsp (30 ml) pickle juice

1 cup (140 g) diced dill pickles

Chopped chives, for garnish (optional)

This is a potato salad like no other. It's made a little differently from most, in that you douse the warm boiled potatoes in a vinaigrette-type mixture before tossing them in the creamy mayonnaise. This adds a ton of extra flavor and makes it really special. Nutty tempeh and diced pickles add to the flavors and textures. It's got a little bit of everything going on; soft, salty, sweet, tangy . . . and I could literally eat the entire bowl myself if it wasn't for others insisting I share!

In a small bowl, combine the vinegar, Dijon mustard, garlic, applesauce, maple syrup, water, ⅛ teaspoon of the salt and the pepper, and whisk together well to form a vinaigrette. Set aside.

Put the cubed potatoes into a large saucepan, cover with water, add the remaining 2 teaspoons (10 g) of salt, bring to a boil, lower the heat to medium-low and allow to simmer until the potatoes are fork-tender. This will take about 5 minutes once the water starts boiling.

Drain well, transfer to a large bowl and immediately, while the potatoes are still hot, pour the vinaigrette over them. Stir to coat the potatoes and allow to cool completely.

While the potatoes are cooling, on a griddle or in a skillet, cook the tempeh strips over medium heat for 3 to 4 minutes on each side, or until golden brown on both sides. If your griddle or skillet is nonstick, you shouldn't need any oil. If it isn't, then use a little oil to prevent it from sticking. Remove from the heat and allow to cool; then chop or crumble into small pieces.

Once the vinaigrette-soaked potatoes are cool, add enough mayonnaise to coat everything nicely. The quantity you need will depend on the consistency of the mayonnaise you use. Then, add the pickle juice and diced pickles, stirring well to combine. Don't worry if the potatoes break up. It only makes it more rustic. Finally, sprinkle with the tempeh pieces and gently stir once more to distribute them—or just leave them on top, if you prefer.

Garnish with chopped chives, if desired, before serving.

tip: *New or baby potatoes are okay to use instead of regular potatoes. Wash them, leave their skins on and cut into bite-size pieces; then cook as directed.*

PIZZA PARTY PULL-APART BREAD

yield: 4 to 6 servings as appetizer or snack

2½ cups (312 g) all-purpose flour, plus more for sprinkling

1¾ tsp (6 g) instant or fast-acting yeast

1⅛ tsp (5.5 g) salt, divided

1½ tsp (6 g) cane or granulated white sugar

About 1 cup (240 ml) lukewarm water, divided

¼ cup (60 ml) olive oil

4 cloves garlic, chopped finely

¼ tsp red pepper flakes

¼ cup (6 g) chopped fresh basil or parsley

⅛ tsp freshly ground black pepper

3 tbsp (24 g) sliced black olives

8 slices vegan pepperoni, quartered

½ to 1 cup (56 to 112 g) shredded vegan mozzarella-style cheese

14 oz (414 ml) pizza sauce

---

tips: *Try dipping the bread in my Mind-Blowing Jalapeño Queso (page 117) instead of pizza sauce, or even better, a bit of both!*

If you forget the pizza sauce, regular tomato ketchup works as a good stand-in!

This recipe was a firm favorite among my recipe testers and family. It's pull-apart bread with all the pizza flavors that you know and love baked right in and is just perfect for parties, get-togethers or for sharing while cozying up on a jammies and movie kind of night. The toppings here are just a guide. As long as you make the bread as written, you can adorn it with whatever you love on your pizzas—just don't forget the pizza sauce for dipping!

In the bowl of a stand mixer or large bowl, whisk together the flour, yeast, 1 teaspoon of the salt and the sugar. Add ¾ cup (180 ml) of the water, while mixing with either the dough hook or a spoon or spatula until it is all starting to combine and most of the dry flour is absorbed. Gradually add the remaining ¼ cup (60 ml) of water to make a dough that is slightly sticky but not really wet when you squeeze it in your hand. If it feels really dry and won't come together, add more water a tablespoon (15 ml) at a time.

Knead it lightly for 5 minutes, either in the stand mixer or by hand (you can do it in the bowl; no need to take it out) until you have a ball of dough that is well formed, slightly sticky, but probably not completely smooth. Cover the bowl with a clean, damp dish towel or plastic wrap and leave to rest for at least 1 hour (up to 5 hours is okay).

When ready to continue, in a small bowl, mix together the olive oil, garlic, red pepper flakes, basil, black pepper and remaining ⅛ teaspoon of salt. Use a little of the oil mixture to brush a 9- to 10-inch (23 to 25.5-cm) ovenproof skillet, cake pan or any similar size ovenproof metal dish.

Sprinkle some flour over the top of the dough and rub some on your hands, too. Break off golf ball–size pieces of dough. Roll them as best you can into balls (they don't have to be perfect) and dip into the oil mixture. Place the balls in the skillet in a single layer, so that they all just gently touch each other. When finished, spoon any remaining oil mixture over them and scatter the olives on top. Tuck the pieces of pepperoni in between the balls.

Leave the pizza bread covered loosely with plastic wrap on the countertop in a draft-free, warm spot for 35 minutes and preheat the oven to 375°F (190°C). After 35 minutes, uncover the bread and sprinkle with the cheese, using as much or as little cheese as you like. Place in the oven and bake for 25 to 30 minutes, or until golden.

Remove from the oven and leave in the pan for 10 minutes before turning it out. While waiting, in a saucepan, warm the pizza sauce gently on the stovetop.

Serve the pizza bread with the sauce for dipping.

GLORIOUSLY GARLICKY PAPRIKA FRIES

yield: 4 servings

2¼ lb (1 kg) potatoes (about 6 large)

¼ cup (60 ml) olive or avocado oil (use aquafaba to make oil-free; see note on page 18), divided

5 cloves garlic, finely chopped

1½ tsp (8 g) salt

1 tsp smoked or regular paprika

1 handful fresh parsley, chopped

Take your homemade fries to the next level because, being without question, the most popular comfort food there is, they (and you) deserve it. Yes, they might take more effort than pulling a bag from the freezer, but every minute you have to wait is so worth it. These taste-bud knock-out fries are golden, perfectly crispy and seasoned with lots *of garlic and paprika. Top them off with a sprinkle of fresh parsley and dig in!*

Preheat the oven to 400°F (200°C).

Peel the potatoes and cut into chunky fries, about ½ inch (1.3 cm) thick and the length of the potatoes. Place in a large saucepan, cover with water and bring to a boil. Allow to boil for 3 minutes; then turn off the heat and drain. They should still be hard. Let them steam dry in the colander and return them to the saucepan.

Pour 2 tablespoons (30 ml) of the oil (or about ¼ cup [60 ml]) aquafaba) over the potatoes, toss to coat well and spread out on a large parchment paper–lined baking sheet (or 2 sheets), making sure they are all in a single layer and there is a little space around each. Bake for 30 minutes.

While they are baking, in a small bowl, mix together the remaining 2 tablespoons (30 ml) of the oil (or 2 tablespoons [30 ml] more of the aquafaba) with the garlic, salt and paprika.

When the 30 minutes are up, remove the fries from the oven and spoon the seasoned oil over them. Use 2 spatulas to toss them all around so there is some oil on each fry. Bake for another 20 to 30 minutes, or until golden brown and crispy.

Sprinkle with the parsley and serve immediately.

tip: *If you are feeling lazy, make a super-quick version with frozen fries. Skip the first couple of steps and bake the fries as directed on the package. Then pick up the recipe from where you prepare the seasoned oil, coat the potatoes and bake again until crispy and golden.*

MIND-BLOWING JALAPEÑO QUESO

yield: 3½ cups (830 ml)

½ medium (400 g) cauliflower, separated into florets

3 cloves garlic, peeled but left whole

1 small (golf ball–size) onion, peeled and quartered

1 jalapeño pepper, left whole but stalk removed

½ heaping cup (70 g) raw cashews

2 tbsp (16 g) tapioca starch or arrowroot powder

½ tsp smoked paprika or chipotle powder

⅛ tsp ground cumin

½ tsp garlic powder

½ tsp onion powder

1 tsp salt, plus more to taste

½ cup (56 g) nutritional yeast (see note on page 49)

2 tbsp (30 ml) white wine vinegar

1¾ cups (420 ml) water

1 tbsp (15 ml) olive oil (optional)

Get ready for your mind to be blown because this queso is crazy good. It's silky smooth, creamy, deliciously cheesy and has a lovely spicy kick. You will want to grab a spoon and delve straight into the blender with reckless abandon. But if you do have superhuman willpower and decide to share, you know what? Served with dippers a-plenty, this queso makes any party better. I absolutely love it with raw broccoli, cauliflower and bell pepper, but it's equally good with crusty baguette, crackers or chips. It reheats perfectly and is really versatile. Use it to make my Whole Enchilada Casserole (page 97), drizzle leftovers over loaded nachos, dollop on veggie burgers or use it as the sauce in a spicy mac and cheese. It's also great in lasagna, casseroles, tacos and burrito bowls.

Preheat the oven to 425°F (218°C). Line a baking sheet with parchment paper.

Place the cauliflower, garlic, onion and jalapeño on the prepared baking sheet (no need to use any oil) and roast for 30 minutes.

While the vegetables are roasting, put the cashews in a small bowl and cover with boiling water. Allow to soak for at least 15 minutes.

Remove the roasted vegetables from the oven and transfer to a blender. Drain the cashews and add them, too, along with all the other ingredients. If you have a small blender, you might need to blend the mixture in two batches. The olive oil is an optional ingredient. It adds a nice sheen to the queso but can easily be omitted if you want to keep the recipe oil-free.

Blend until completely smooth, and pour into a saucepan. Heat over medium heat, stirring constantly, until thick, glossy and hot, about 10 minutes. If it gets a little too thick, dilute with a little water. Check the seasoning and add more salt, if necessary.

Can be served hot, warm or cold.

a tip for the brave: *This queso is nicely spicy without being really hot. If you like things really spicy, use two jalapeño peppers instead of one.*

SMASH-'EM-UP SALT AND VINEGAR POTATOES

yield: 3 or 4 servings

1½ lb (680 g) baby potatoes, peel on

1¼ cups (300 ml) white vinegar, divided

2 tsp (10 g) salt

3 tbsp (45 ml) olive oil

Sea salt flakes, for sprinkling

It's time to change up your roasties! As a family, we are obsessed with potatoes no matter how they are cooked, but roasted potatoes are probably my favorite. Second best are fries with lots of salt and vinegar. So, I decided to combine the two and make myself, and you, very happy. Once you add the vinegar and flaky sea salt, the hot, smashed, crispy potatoes become absolutely addictive. The smashing part, as well as being satisfying to do, makes them even better. It is extremely hard not to eat them all straight off the pan, but if they do escape your clutches, they make a great side, snack or appetizer and go down very well at parties.

Preheat the oven to 450°F (232°C).

Put the potatoes in a saucepan. Pour 1 cup (240 ml) of the vinegar over them, and add the salt. Top up with enough cold water to just cover the potatoes. Bring to a boil and cook for about 7 minutes, or until you can just insert a fork into them but they aren't yet cooked through. Drain immediately and let sit in the colander for a few minutes to steam dry.

Return the potatoes to the saucepan you boiled them in and toss with the olive oil; then spread out on a large baking sheet in a single layer with room between each potato. Bake for 30 minutes, and then remove from the oven. Smash each potato with a potato masher or the bottom of a mug so it flattens and splits. Drizzle with the remaining ¼ cup (60 ml) of vinegar, making sure to do it as evenly as you can. Then return the pan to the oven and bake again for about another 30 minutes, or until really golden and crispy.

Sprinkle with a generous scattering of flaky sea salt and serve immediately.

MIRACLE NO-KNEAD FOCACCIA

yield: 9 servings

4 cups (500 g) all-purpose flour or bread flour

1 tbsp (10 g) instant or fast-acting yeast

2 tsp (10 g) salt

5 tbsp (75 ml) olive oil, divided

1¾ cups plus 2 tbsp (450 ml) cold water

2 tbsp (3 g) fresh or dried rosemary

Sea salt flakes or crystals, for scattering

tip: *It is really important to use the correct amount of flour in this recipe. I really recommend weighing it, but if you can't, measure the cups by spooning the flour into the cups and leveling off with the back of a knife—do not scoop and do not compact the flour by pressing down on it as you fill the cup.*

This is officially the easiest bread recipe ever and is virtually foolproof. No kneading or shaping is involved at all. All you have to do is stir and wait. The only skill necessary is patience. I love just about any bread that's served warm right from the oven, but there's something extra-special about comforting, olive oil–rich focaccia kicked up a notch with a generous amount of rosemary and sea salt. It really is a treat and makes a great accompaniment to pasta, salads, chili, soups and stews. Leftovers make wicked panini or toasted sandwiches, too. If you aren't a bread baker, hold tight, because you are about to become one!

In a large mixing bowl, combine the flour, yeast and salt; then add 1 tablespoon (15 ml) of the olive oil. Add the water and mix well, making sure you scrape right down to the bottom of the bowl, until you can see no more dry flour and you have a wet, slightly lumpy-looking mess. Cover with plastic wrap or a clean, damp dish towel and leave on the kitchen counter for a minimum of 7 hours and a maximum of 9 hours. Do not refrigerate and do not leave anywhere really warm. Just normal room temperature is fine.

About 20 minutes before the time is up, preheat your oven to 400°F (200°C) and line an 8-inch (20.5-cm) square pan or a 9-inch (23-cm) round, deep cake pan with a large square of parchment paper. There is no need to get fancy. Just push it into the pan so it fits in snugly, making sure there is some coming up and over the sides to enable you to lift the loaf out later.

When the oven is at temperature, scrape the dough from the bowl and into the prepared pan. It will be clingy and sticky. A dough scraper or stiff spatula makes the job easier. Once it's all in the pan, flatten it out so it's as even all over as you can get it. Then, using a finger dipped in olive oil, make dimples all over the top.

Drizzle with the remaining olive oil (you can add more if you want it ultra-decadently olive oil–y) and sprinkle the rosemary evenly over the top along with some flaky salt. Bake for 37 to 40 minutes, or until the dough is slightly golden across the top and edges, fluffy and cooked through.

Remove from the oven, lift out using the paper as handles and place on a cooling rack. Serve hot, warm or cold.

"ALE, YEAH" ROSEMARY ONION BEER BREAD

yield: 10 to 12 slices

2 tsp (10 ml) olive oil or water

1 medium onion, sliced into thin half-moons

2 tbsp (24 g) cane or granulated white sugar, divided

2 tbsp (30 ml) melted vegan butter, divided (optional)

3 cups (375 g) all-purpose flour

3 cloves garlic, finely chopped

1½ tsp (1 g) very finely chopped fresh rosemary (about two 2" [5-cm] sprigs)

1 tsp salt

1 tbsp (12 g) baking powder

¼ tsp freshly ground black pepper

12 oz (354 ml) beer or ale

Yes, we are making quick bread with beer and it's so good! There is no yeast involved and once the onion is sautéed, it takes mere minutes to mix up and pop into the oven. The flavor is amazing and the crumb is incredibly soft and fluffy, thanks to the bubbly, foaming beer. Eating it warm from the oven, dripping with my Life-Changing Vegan Butter (page 188), is a comfort food experience not to be missed. Serve it as it is, pack it in lunch boxes, use as an appetizer with a vegan cheese board or as a side with soups and stews. I advise you double the recipe and make two because the first will be gone in minutes!

In a small skillet, heat the olive oil or water (for oil-free cooking) over medium heat. Add the onion and 1 tablespoon (12 g) of the sugar. Cook, stirring frequently, for about 15 minutes, or until really golden and caramelized. If using water to sauté, add a little more throughout the cooking process to prevent sticking. Remove from the heat and allow to cool.

Meanwhile, preheat the oven to 375°F (190°C) and grease a 9 x 5-inch (23 x 12.5-cm) loaf pan with a little of the melted vegan butter or oil spray. If your loaf pan doesn't release easily, line it with a strip of baking parchment lengthwise down the middle, with enough to go up and over the ends to act as handles.

In a bowl, combine the remaining tablespoon (12 g) of sugar, the flour, garlic, rosemary, salt, baking powder and pepper, and mix well. Add the cooled onion and beer. The batter will bubble up and fizz. Stir gently, just enough so that everything is combined. Do not overmix.

Spoon into the prepared pan, drizzle with the optional remaining melted butter and place in the oven. Bake for 40 to 45 minutes or until a toothpick or knife inserted into the middle of the loaf comes out clean. Remove from the pan and let cool on a cooling rack.

Great eaten while still warm or when cold.

tips: *Try scattering some vegan cheese over the top before baking!*

Uncut loaves can be wrapped well and frozen for up to 2 months.

THERE'S NO SUCH THING AS TOO MUCH GARLIC BREAD

yield: 8 servings

5 tbsp (75 ml) unsweetened nondairy milk

1 tsp nutritional yeast (see note on page 49)

½ tsp salt

½ tsp apple cider vinegar

2 tbsp (30 ml) olive oil

½ cup (120 ml) melted refined coconut oil (it must be refined)

Pinch of ground turmeric (optional; for color only)

5 large cloves garlic, chopped very finely or pressed through a garlic press

1 to 2 tbsp (4 to 8 g) finely chopped fresh parsley

1 or 2 pinches of red pepper flakes

8 slices crusty vegan bread

If you have made my Life-Changing Vegan Butter (page 188), you will know how delicious it is, and this is a riff on that recipe. With a little adaption, it makes the most amazing garlic "butter," which in turn makes the most completely, utterly, insanely delicious garlic bread that takes no time at all to whip up. It's hot, crisp, golden, toasty, drippy and packs one serious flavor punch! Serve it alongside pasta, chili, soups or salads—or just enjoy it on its own.

In a blender, combine the nondairy milk, nutritional yeast, salt, vinegar, olive oil, coconut oil and turmeric (if using) and blend until well mixed. Transfer to a small bowl and add the garlic, parsley and red pepper flakes. Allow to sit for at least 10 minutes for the garlic to infuse the "butter."

Place the slices of bread on a baking sheet and broil on medium (about 400°F [200°C]) on one side until golden and toasty. Remove the pan from the oven and turn over the slices of bread so the unbroiled side is upward. Give the garlic "butter" a quick stir, and then spoon it over the slices really generously. Do it slowly so it has time to seep in and not run over the sides too much.

Broil until bubbling and golden. Watch the edges of the bread and remove just before they turn from dark golden brown to black! Don't leave them unattended as this can happen very quickly!

tips: *Use a baguette instead. Cut it in half lengthwise and spoon garlic "butter" over both sides, allowing it to seep in before putting the baguette back together again and wrapping tightly in aluminum foil. Bake at 400°F (200°C) for 15 minutes. Remove, unwrap carefully and cut into generous wedges.*

Leftover garlic "butter" will keep in a sealed container in the fridge for up to 2 weeks. It also freezes well. It will solidify when it chills and might separate a little. Just melt it gently, stir and use as desired. It can be used in any way you would use regular garlic butter. Try it for sautéing, on baked potatoes, new potatoes, mashed potatoes or corn, in pasta dishes or on green beans. It's also great used in place of the butter in my "Ale, Yeah" Rosemary Onion Beer Bread (page 122).

QUICK AND CRISPY ZUCCHINI FRITTERS WITH AVOCADO CREMA

yield: 8 fritters

fritters

3 medium zucchini

1 medium onion

1½ tsp (8 g) salt

½ tsp ground cumin

1 tsp dried oregano

1 tsp dried thyme

3 cloves garlic, finely chopped

2 tbsp (14 g) ground flaxseeds

Zest of 1 small lemon (reserve the rest of the lemon for the crema)

1½ cups (138 g) garbanzo bean flour

1½ tsp (6 g) baking powder

½ tsp red pepper flakes (optional)

Olive or vegetable oil, for pan

These fritters are super simple and easy to make. They're crispy on the outside and moist but not soggy on the inside. They make great party food, appetizers or snacks and are also perfect for a more substantial dinner with salad, or in a bun in place of a burger. No matter how you stack them, though, one thing is certain: When it comes to crispy fritters straight from the pan, just one is not enough!

To prepare the fritters, grate the zucchini and onion. If you have a food processor, use the grating attachment to do this, which makes it really quick and easy. Transfer to a bowl, sprinkle with the salt, stir really well and leave for at least 30 minutes; longer is okay.

Transfer the mixture to a large sieve or colander and use clean hands to press out the water; alternatively, wrap in a clean dish towel and wring out the water. It is important to get as much water out as possible.

Return the mixture to the bowl. Add the cumin, oregano, thyme, garlic, flaxseeds, lemon zest, garbanzo flour, baking powder and red pepper flakes (if using). Stir together really well so everything is distributed well and you cannot see any dry flour. It will be a very stiff batter. Leave it to rest for 10 minutes. During this time, it will loosen up a little.

Heat a griddle or large skillet over medium heat. Grease with a little oil if it's not nonstick. Once it's hot, give the batter a quick stir, and then add it to the pan, using around ⅓ cup (80 ml) per fritter and leaving about 2 inches (5 cm) around each one. Use a spoon to flatten the fritters to about ½ inch (1.3 cm) thick and allow to cook for about 7 minutes each side, or until golden brown. Serve them immediately or keep warm in the oven on its lowest setting while you finish cooking the rest.

You can also bake the fritters in a preheated 400°F (200°C) oven. Line a baking sheet with parchment paper and drop the mixture onto it in roughly ⅓-cup (80-ml) amounts; then flatten them to about ½ inch (1.3 cm) thick. Bake for 10 to 15 minutes, flip them and then bake for an additional 10 minutes.

(continued)

avocado crema

1 medium avocado

3 tbsp (45 ml) fresh lemon juice

1 clove garlic

1 tsp sriracha or other hot sauce

2 tsp (10 ml) white wine vinegar

5 tbsp (75 ml) water

2 tbsp (30 ml) olive oil (optional)

Salt

To prepare the avocado crema, cut the avocado in half. Remove the pit and scoop out the flesh into a blender or food processor. Add all the other crema ingredients except the salt and blend until completely smooth. Season with salt to taste. You can adjust the thickness by adding a little more or less water. The olive oil is an optional addition. It makes the crema glossier, but you can easily omit it and add 1 to 2 tablespoons (15 to 30 ml) of extra water instead.

Serve the hot fritters with a generous dollop of avocado crema.

Leftover fritters keep well for up to 5 days in the fridge. They also freeze really well. They can be reheated in a skillet over medium heat or in the oven. They are also surprisingly good cold! The crema will keep in a sealed container in the fridge for 2 to 3 days.

tip: Enjoy leftover crema as a dip with chips, with tacos, burritos, veggie burgers and sandwiches or thin it out with a little more water or a drop of white wine vinegar to make a great salad dressing!

"KALE CAESAR!" PASTA SALAD

yield: 8 to 10 servings

croutons

½ large loaf (about 12 oz [350 g]) vegan bread that is a couple of days old

2 tbsp (30 ml) olive or avocado oil (optional)

¾ tsp salt

½ tsp freshly ground black pepper

16 oz (454 g) of your favorite dry pasta shapes

1 tbsp (15 ml) olive oil (optional)

dressing

1 cup (140 g) raw cashews

½ tsp Dijon mustard

4 cloves garlic

2 tbsp (30 ml) white wine vinegar

1 tsp salt

½ tsp freshly ground black pepper

¼ cup (28 g) nutritional yeast (see note on page 49)

2 tbsp (30 ml) fresh lemon juice

1 cup (240 ml) water

¼ slightly heaping cup (34 g) capers

3 tbsp (45 ml) olive or avocado oil (optional)

Kale. It has a bad rep. But when done right, it can be amazing and that's exactly what the deal is here. The tough stems are removed and the deep green leaves are massaged in a salty, tangy, "cheesy" Caesar dressing until tender. Then, it's mixed with pasta, drowned in more of that delicious, creamy dressing and topped with crunchy croutons (substitute store-bought if in a hurry) and a hefty scattering of vegan "Parmesan." This is a book filled with vegan comfort food and healthy, superfood salads don't belong, but one as carb-loaded, creamy, cheesy and delicious as this can make it in with head held high. Trust me. I had some kale skeptics among my recipe testers and every single one of them adored this!

First, prepare the croutons. Preheat the oven to 375°F (190°C); then cut the bread into ¾-inch (2-cm) cubes. In a large bowl, toss the bread cubes with the olive oil, salt and pepper. You can omit the oil and they will still crisp up, but they won't taste quite as good. Spread out the croutons in a single layer on a baking sheet and bake for 10 minutes. Then turn them all over and return to the oven until golden and crispy. It should take about another 10 minutes, but if you cut your bread bigger or smaller, the time will change a little. Remove from the oven and let cool on the tray completely; then store in an airtight container. They should keep well for up to 2 weeks.

Cook the pasta according to the package directions, drain and immediately rinse in cold water, shake to remove as much water as possible, transfer back to the saucepan, add the olive oil and stir to coat. This will help prevent the pasta from sticking together. Set aside. If you want the recipe to be oil-free, just drain and rinse and omit the olive oil.

Prepare the dressing. In a blender, combine the dressing ingredients, except the capers, and blend for a minute or two until completely smooth. If you decide to omit the oil, add an extra 3 tablespoons (45 ml) of water instead.

(continued)

"KALE CAESAR!" PASTA SALAD (CONTINUED)

1 bunch kale (about 7 large leaves or 450 g), stemmed and chopped into bite-size pieces

Cheesy Brazil Nut "Parm" (page 191), or store-bought vegan Parmesan, for serving

Put the kale in a large salad bowl and spoon ¼ cup (60 ml) of the dressing over it. With clean hands, begin massaging the kale. Do this for 4 to 5 minutes. Really squeeze it and rub it together between your fingers. It sounds crazy, but bear with me! You will start with a really full bowl but as you massage, the kale will more than halve in volume and become smoother, much more tender and lighter in color.

Add the cooked pasta to the massaged kale; add the capers to the remaining dressing and pour it over the pasta and kale. Stir really well, making sure everything is coated with the dressing.

Top with the croutons and a sprinkling of my Cheesy Brazil Nut "Parm," if desired.

The pasta salad will keep for 2 to 3 days in the fridge. It might dry out a little, but just add a few tablespoons of water and give it a good stir before serving and it will be good as new.

The croutons and "Parm" are best added at the time of serving so that they keep their texture.

tips: If you are a kale hater, use a head of romaine lettuce instead and skip the massaging bit. Leftovers won't keep as well as they do when using kale, though.

The dressing is also great made on its own for serving with regular leafy salads or for making a more traditional Caesar salad too.

DOWN 'N' DIRTY TACO FRIES

yield: 4 servings

fries

2¼ lb (1 kg) large white potatoes

½ cup (120 ml) aquafaba (the liquid from the can of chickpeas used for the topping below), or 3 tbsp (45 ml) olive oil

3 tbsp (8 g) taco seasoning

1 tsp salt

topping

1 (15-oz [425-g]) can chickpeas, drained (reserve the liquid for the fries above)

2 large, juicy fresh tomatoes, chopped (try to keep as much as possible of their juices)

½ medium red onion, finely chopped

1 lime

2 tbsp (30 ml) olive oil (optional)

lime crema

⅓ heaping cup (50 g) raw cashews, soaked for 15 minutes in boiling water, then drained

About ⅓ cup + 2 tbsp (113 ml) water, divided

Zest and juice of 1 lime

1 tbsp (15 ml) pure maple syrup

½ tsp salt

⅛ tsp freshly ground black pepper

Whip up a platter of these loaded fries, gather up your friends and family and prepare for things to get messy. The combo of hot, spicy fries; cool, fresh topping and zesty lime crema is so good!

Preheat the oven to 450°F (232°C). Line a large baking sheet with parchment paper.

Prepare the fries. If the potatoes have thin, clean-looking skin, just give them a good wash. If the skin is thick and dirty looking, peel them. Then, cut each potato into fries about ½ inch (1.3 cm) thick. Place in a large pan, cover with water and bring to a boil. As soon as the water starts to boil, after 10 to 15 minutes, turn off the heat and drain. This must be done immediately. They need to remain quite hard; don't let them get soft. Return the fries to the pan and leave them, lid off, for about 5 minutes to steam dry.

Pour the aquafaba, or oil if you prefer, over the fries, and then sprinkle with the taco seasoning and salt. Stir gently and ensure each individual fry is covered well before gently tipping out onto the prepared baking sheet. Spread out evenly into a single layer with a little space around each fry to ensure ultimate crispness.

Bake for 30 minutes; then remove from the oven, turn all the fries over carefully and return them to the oven for a further 20 to 30 minutes. They should be golden and crispy. If you use oil instead of aquafaba, they will bake slightly quicker, so keep a careful eye on them in the final 20 minutes of baking time.

Meanwhile, prepare the topping. Place the drained chickpeas in a bowl. Add the tomatoes, their juices and the red onion. Grate the zest from the lime—then juice it and add both to the chickpea mixture along with the olive oil (if using). Stir really well and set aside.

Prepare the crema. In a blender, combine the drained cashews and 5 tablespoons (75 ml) of the fresh water. Add the lime zest and juice along with the maple syrup, salt and pepper. Blend until completely smooth. If you prefer a slightly thinner crema, add the rest of the water gradually, pulsing in between until you get a good thick, but drizzlable consistency.

Once the fries are cooked, remove them from the oven and pile them onto individual plates or a platter. Spoon the chickpea topping over the top of the fries along with any juices in the bottom of the bowl. Then drizzle with a generous amount of lime crema.

sweet talk

I have the biggest sweet tooth, and for me, sometimes (okay, nearly all of the time) the dessert is better than the main event. I just adore sweet treats of all kinds. I always feel let down when I go out to eat at restaurants and there is no vegan dessert option, especially when all of my nonvegan friends are tucking into something that looks amazing.

But never fear! This chapter is dedicated to your sweet tooth and it is full of comforting, heartwarming desserts that include all your favorites, including cake, cheesecake, pie and sticky puddings. Your days of going without a delicious dessert are numbered.

Ready for some sweet talk? Then, follow me . . . and be prepared to swoon.

DREAMY BAKED BERRY CHEESECAKE

yield: 10 servings

fruit sauce

3 cups (454 g) frozen berries (any type, but a mixture is nice)

½ cup (100 g) granulated white or cane sugar

1 tbsp (15 ml) fresh lemon juice

crust

Vegan butter or oil, for pan

12 oz (350 g) digestive biscuits or graham crackers (about 27 digestive biscuits or 23 graham crackers)

¼ cup (60 ml) melted vegan butter or coconut oil

The perfect crowd-pleasing dessert. With a crisp, crumbly, buttery crust; a thick layer of rich, creamy, velvety filling; a simple, yet amazing fruit sauce, and piles of fresh berries, it is impossible to deny this cheesecakes decadence. Trust me when it comes to the chickpeas. Yes, it's a very odd addition, but they are my trick for getting that perfect, tenderly firm, New York cheesecake texture. If you don't admit it, no one will ever guess they are there! This is an adapted version of a cheesecake recipe that is on my blog and it is one of my most popular recipes. I can't wait for you to try it!

First, prepare the fruit sauce. In a saucepan, combine the frozen berries with the sugar and lemon juice. Warm over medium heat for about 10 minutes, stirring occasionally, until the berries are soft and defrosted and the sugar has dissolved. Transfer to a blender and blend until smooth; then strain through a sieve to remove any seeds. Return the sauce to the pan and, over medium heat, allow it to reduce by about one quarter. This will take about 15 minutes. Remove from the heat and allow to cool. Transfer to a sealed container and refrigerate. It will thicken up nicely once chilled.

Preheat the oven to 325°F (162°C). Grease the bottom and sides of an 8- or 9-inch (20.5- or 23-cm) springform pan with a little vegan butter or oil; then line it with a circle of parchment paper on the bottom and a strip around the sides. The butter or oil helps keep the paper in place.

To prepare the crust, in a food processor, process the biscuits until they are fine crumbs. Pour in the melted vegan butter or coconut oil and process until combined. Spoon out into the prepared pan and press down really hard all over to compact the crumbs evenly into the bottom. Put the pan in the fridge or freezer while you make the filling.

(continued)

filling

2¾ cups (400 g) raw cashews

1 cup (240 g) canned chickpeas, drained and rinsed well

Zest and juice of 1 lemon

1 tbsp (15 ml) vanilla extract

2 tbsp (16 g) arrowroot powder or cornstarch

½ cup (120 ml) pure maple syrup

2 tbsp (30 g) tahini or cashew butter

1 (13.5-oz [400-ml]) can full-fat coconut milk

½ tsp salt

3 tbsp (45 ml) apple cider vinegar

Fresh berries of choice, for topping

For the filling, pour boiling water over the cashews and allow to soak for at least 15 minutes. Don't skip this step, even if you have a high-powered blender. It helps make the filling extra-smooth and velvety.

In a blender, combine the chickpeas, lemon zest and juice, vanilla, arrowroot powder, maple syrup, tahini, coconut milk, salt and vinegar. Drain the cashews, discarding the water, and add them to the blender, too. Blend it all up until creamy and completely smooth.

Remove the crust from the fridge and pour in the filling. Place on a baking sheet in the oven and bake for about 50 minutes. The filling should be set around the edges with a slight wobble in the middle. Turn off the oven, crack open the oven door and allow the cheesecake to cool in there for about 1 hour before removing. If you need the oven for something else or you aren't able to have the door slightly open, you can remove the cheesecake immediately, but you risk some cracks appearing in the top. They will be covered with sauce and fruit anyway, so it isn't too much of a problem. Once the cheesecake has cooled completely, cover the pan tightly with plastic wrap and chill for at least 4 hours before serving.

Remove the cheesecake from the pan, place on a serving plate and spoon a generous amount of the chilled fruit sauce on top. Use a spatula to spread it out evenly over the surface. Top with piles of fresh berries and serve sliced with the remaining sauce.

The cheesecake can be stored covered in the fridge for up to 1 week.

tips: *Leftover fruit sauce is great with ice cream, oatmeal, pancakes (page 28) or French toast (page 23).*

For an alternative topping, use the cherry sauce from my Black Forest Breakfast Crepes (page 17) or the toffee sauce from my Sinfully Sticky Toffee Pudding (page 142).

JAM-TASTIC VICTORIA SPONGE CAKE

yield: 8 to 10 slices

sponge

½ cup (110 g) vegan butter, plus more for the pan

3 cups + heaping ¼ cup (410 g) all-purpose flour

1 tsp salt

1 tsp baking soda

2 tsp (8 g) baking powder

6 tbsp (90 ml) aquafaba (see note on page 18)

4 tsp (20 ml) vanilla extract

2 tbsp (30 ml) apple cider vinegar (see note on page 38)

1½ cups (360 ml) unsweetened nondairy milk

1 cup (200 g) cane or granulated white sugar

There's just something about a good old Victoria sponge cake. It's classic and simple and usually pretty reserved, but this is my version, and when it comes to desserts, I'm far from reserved. We are going all out here with a thick layer of buttercream and copious amounts of dribbly, sticky jam, sandwiched between two layers of super-fluffy, "buttery" sponge. Then, it's all finished off with a very generous drift of powdered sugar. It's vegan (but you'd never know), it's jam-tastic and it's the perfect cake to add to your comfort food repertoire!

To prepare the sponge, preheat the oven to 350°F (180°C). Grease two 8-inch (20.5-cm) round regular or springform cake pans with a little vegan butter and lay a round piece of baking parchment in the bottom of each. This makes the cake removal really easy. To cut to the right size, you can place the pan or its loose bottom insert on the parchment paper and draw around it—then cut to fit.

Sift the flour into a bowl and whisk in the salt, baking soda and baking powder.

In a separate small bowl, whisk together the aquafaba, vanilla, vinegar and nondairy milk.

In the bowl of a stand mixer fitted with the paddle attachment, beat the vegan butter and sugar together for a good 3 to 4 minutes, or until light and fluffy. Alternatively, an electric hand mixer also works well, or you can do it by hand. Don't be tempted to rush this step as it really helps the texture of the sponge.

Pour the flour mixture into the butter mixture; then start mixing on low speed, while gradually adding the aquafaba mixture. If working by hand, stir well after each addition.

Do not overmix the batter. Just continue until there is no dry flour visible and most of the lumps are out. A few small ones are fine. The batter should be velvety and thick.

Divide the batter evenly between the prepared cake pans, and bake for 32 to 35 minutes. The sponge should be coming away from the edges of the pan and if you press gently in the middle with a finger, it should spring back. A toothpick inserted into the middle of the cake should come out clean.

(continued)

JAM-TASTIC VICTORIA SPONGE CAKE (CONTINUED)

filling

½ cup + 1 tbsp (124 g) vegan butter

1 tsp vanilla extract

Small pinch of salt

1¾ cups (210 g) powdered sugar, plus more for dusting

½ cup (120 ml) good-quality strawberry or raspberry jam

Turn out each sponge onto a cooling rack and peel the baking parchment off the bottoms. Leave to cool completely before attempting to assemble or frost.

For the filling, in a bowl, beat the vegan butter with the vanilla and salt until soft and fluffy. Then, gradually add the powdered sugar, mixing well between each addition. Place in the fridge to firm up for about 20 minutes before trying to frost the cake.

To assemble the cake, saving the sponge layer that looks best for the top, place one of the sponges upside down on a plate so the flat side is facing upward. If it is very domed, you might need to trim a tiny piece off the underside with a bread knife to prevent it from wobbling. I tend to find, though, that by the time everything is added on top, the weight makes it stable.

Gently spread the buttercream evenly on this bottom layer, working from the middle out. If you have trouble spreading it, dip your spatula into some water; it will make it go on much smoother. Then, add the jam in an even layer before placing the second sponge gently on top.

Dust the top of the cake with a generous sprinkling of powdered sugar, using a shaker or a small sieve.

tips: Don't be tempted to substitute any other vegan egg replacement for the aquafaba in this recipe. It really is the best option for this cake and gives much better results than any other egg substitute.

Need a celebration cake? Try making extra frosting to cover the top and outside of the cake. Then decorate with piping or decorations of choice.

SINFULLY STICKY TOFFEE PUDDING

yield: 8 servings

pudding

⅓ cup (80 ml) melted vegan butter or coconut oil, plus more for the pan

12 Medjool dates (about 6 oz [170 g]), pitted and chopped very small

1 cup (240 ml) freshly made, hot, strong black coffee

1 slightly heaping tsp baking soda

1 tbsp (15 ml) vanilla extract

2⅓ cups (270 g) spelt flour, 2 cups + 2 tbsp (270 g) all-purpose flour or 3 cups (270 g) oat flour (spelt gives the best result)

¾ cup (165 g) dark brown sugar or coconut sugar

1½ tsp (6 g) baking powder

½ tsp ground cinnamon

½ tsp salt

⅓ cup (82 g) applesauce or mashed banana (if you don't mind a banana flavor coming through)

This is the kind of warm sponge pudding that gets served in British country pubs after Sunday lunch and it's one of my favorites. It's dark, sweet, rich, naughty and satisfying. Don't be put off by the dates. This doesn't taste "healthy" in the slightest. They dissolve almost completely into the sponge and are what gives the pudding its moist, rich, sticky sweetness. Then once it's baked, you rather satisfyingly poke holes all over the pudding and douse it in toffee sauce so it seeps right into the sponge, making it even more ridiculously sticky and indulgent. Stretchy pants are optional but recommended.

Prepare the pudding. Preheat the oven to 350°F (176°C). Grease 8 small individual pudding molds, 8 wells of a muffin pan or an 8-inch (20.5-cm) square cake pan with a little vegan butter or coconut oil. Then line the bottoms with a little circle or square of parchment paper. The butter or oil helps keep it in place.

Place the dates in a medium bowl and pour the brewed coffee over them. Add the baking soda and vanilla; stir and set aside.

In a large bowl, whisk together the flour, sugar, baking powder, cinnamon and salt.

Add the melted vegan butter or oil and the applesauce to the date mixture and stir to combine. Then pour it into the flour mixture and fold together until just combined. Do not overmix.

Divide the batter equally between the 8 prepared pudding molds or wells, or spoon all of the batter into the prepared pan. If you used individual pudding molds, set them on a baking sheet so they will stay level in the oven. Bake for 25 minutes, or until a toothpick inserted into the center of a pudding comes out clean.

(continued)

sauce

1 cup (220 g) dark brown sugar or coconut sugar

1 cup (240 ml) full-fat canned coconut milk

2 tbsp (28 g) vegan butter (optional)

¼ tsp salt

¼ cup (32 g) chopped pecans or walnuts

While the puddings are baking, prepare the sauce. In a small saucepan, combine the brown sugar, coconut milk, vegan butter, if using, and the salt. The butter helps make it richer, so it is recommended. Allow to come to a gentle boil over medium heat. Keep it bubbling away, stirring frequently right into the bottom to make sure it doesn't burn, until it can coat the back of a metal spoon. It will still appear thin but will thicken as it cools. Remove from the heat.

Remove the puddings from the oven and immediately poke them all over with a sharp, thin knife. With care, as the sauce will be very hot, pour 1 tablespoon (15 ml) of the toffee sauce over the top of each pudding, or ½ cup (120 ml) if a single pan was used. At first, it will pool on the top but will slowly sink in. At this point you can serve them or allow them to cool, wrap in plastic wrap and either refrigerate or freeze.

To serve, run a knife around the edges of each pudding and turn them out onto individual plates or bowls, or divide into 8 portions. Add the chopped pecans to the sauce and spoon a generous amount over each pudding.

To make the puddings extra-sticky and chewy, turn them out, pour some sauce over them and broil the tops for a couple of minutes, until they are bubbling and crusty.

Leftover sauce will keep in the fridge for up to 1 week. It also freezes well.

tips: Puddings will keep well in the freezer for up to 3 months. Reheat in the oven straight from frozen on 350°F (176°C) for 15 to 20 minutes.

For a special treat, add a couple tablespoons of rum, brandy or bourbon to the toffee sauce.

CRAZY GOOD CARROT CUPCAKES

yield: 8 large cupcakes

cupcakes

Oil, for pan (optional)

¾ cup (94 g) all-purpose flour

¾ slightly heaping cup (86 g) spelt flour

2 tsp (8 g) baking powder

Slightly heaping ½ tsp baking soda

½ cup (100 g) coconut sugar or light brown sugar

2 tsp (5 g) ground cinnamon

¼ tsp ground nutmeg

½ tsp salt

¼ cup (40 g) golden raisins or sultanas

2 tbsp (16 g) chopped pecans or walnuts

½ cup (90 g) diced canned or fresh pineapple

1 cup (110 g) grated carrot

⅓ cup (82 g) unsweetened applesauce or pureed cooked sweet potato

¼ cup (60 ml) unsweetened nondairy milk

1½ tsp (8 ml) vanilla extract

⅓ cup (80 ml) liquid coconut oil or any other mildly flavored oil

1 tsp apple cider vinegar (see note on page 38)

This is my favorite way to get a serving of vegetables! Without the decadent frosting, these cupcakes could easily morph into muffins. They are certainly hearty enough, but combined with the frosting, they are absolutely crazy good. Like, ridiculously so. In fact, if I was forced to choose, this might be my favorite recipe in the entire book. The cupcakes are packed with wholesome carrots, fruit, nuts and spices and they have the perfect soft, fluffy texture. The frosting is sweet and creamy with a slight cream cheese tang and turns them from ordinary muffin-ness to decadent cupcake-ness with one quick squeeze of the piping bag. Combining spelt and all-purpose flour gives the very best results, but you can use all all-purpose or all spelt if you prefer.

To prepare the cupcakes, preheat the oven to 350°F (176°C) and grease or line 8 wells of a muffin pan.

In a large bowl, whisk together the flours, baking powder, baking soda, sugar, cinnamon, nutmeg and salt. Then add the raisins and nuts and give a quick stir.

Squeeze as much juice as you can from the pineapple. You can do it by squeezing it in your fist or in a sieve with a spoon to press it with. You need just the squeezed-out flesh and not the juice. Save the juice for a smoothie or just drink it.

In a medium bowl, combine the pineapple pulp with the carrot, applesauce, nondairy milk, vanilla, oil and vinegar. Give it all a good mix, and then pour it into the flour mixture. Mix until you can't see any dry flour, but don't overmix.

Spoon the batter evenly into the prepared muffin pan and bake for 30 to 35 minutes, or until a toothpick inserted into the middle of a cupcake comes out clean. Remove from the oven, place on a cooling rack and allow to cool completely before attempting to frost.

(continued)

frosting

½ cup (113 g) vegan cream cheese

¼ cup (55 g) vegan butter

2 tsp (5 g) arrowroot powder or cornstarch

Pinch of salt

1 tsp vanilla extract

1½ to 2 cups (195 to 260 g) powdered sugar

For the frosting, in a bowl, beat together the vegan cream cheese, vegan butter, arrowroot powder, salt and vanilla until they are combined and just fluffy. Don't overbeat, as they will get too melty. Gradually add the powdered sugar, about ½ cup (65 g) at a time, beating between each addition. If you just want to spread the frosting on the cupcakes, 1½ cups (195 g) of powdered sugar is sufficient, but if you want to pipe it, you will need to add a total of 2 cups (260 g) so it is a little stiffer. Refrigerate for at least 30 minutes to let it firm up before spreading or piping onto each cupcake. The frosting will keep for up to 5 days in the fridge if you want to make it in advance.

tips: *Grate a little too much carrot, accidently on purpose, and spread out about 2 tablespoons (14 g) of it on a parchment paper–lined baking sheet, then bake in a 300°F (150°C) oven for 20 minutes, or until it dries out. Keep an eye on it toward the end in case it starts darkening too much. Once it cools, it will be brittle enough for you to crumble up with your fingers to make carrot "sprinkles." Sprinkle them over the top of the frosted cupcakes for decoration like mine!*

Make a loaf instead of cupcakes! Bake in a 9 x 5–inch (23 x 12.5–cm) loaf pan in a 350°F (176°C) oven for about 50 minutes.

DROOL-WORTHY CINNAMON DONUTS

yield: 6 donuts

Vegan butter or coconut oil, for pan

1 cup + 3 tbsp (150 g) all-purpose flour

½ cup (100 g) cane or granulated white sugar

1¼ tsp (5 g) baking powder

⅛ tsp baking soda

¼ tsp salt

¼ tsp ground cinnamon

¼ tsp ground nutmeg

2 tsp (10 ml) vanilla extract

1 tbsp (15 ml) apple cider vinegar (see note on page 38)

½ cup + 3 tbsp (165 ml) canned light coconut milk

There is nothing quite like fresh, warm donuts, and with this recipe, you get perfectly soft and fluffy donuts with no deep-frying. They are baked in the oven, but by the time they have been dipped in melted vegan butter, and rolled in their warming, comforting cinnamon-y sugary coating, they taste as if they had been fried. If you cook oil-free, I give instructions for how to make them without the butter; and if you don't own a donut pan, don't worry. You can bake them as muffins or as donut holes in a mini muffin pan instead.

Preheat the oven to 350°F (176°C) and grease 6 wells of a donut pan with a little vegan butter or coconut oil.

Sift the flour into a bowl. Add the sugar, baking powder, baking soda, salt, cinnamon and nutmeg; then whisk together to combine.

In another bowl, combine the vanilla, vinegar and coconut milk. Stir them together, and pour into the flour mixture. Gently stir until all of the flour is absorbed and you can no longer see any dry flour. Do not overmix or beat the batter. It will be a thick batter.

Spoon carefully and evenly into the prepared donut pan and level/tidy up the batter with the back of a teaspoon.

Bake for 12 to 15 minutes, or until the donuts are coming away from the edge of the pan and a toothpick inserted into a donut comes out clean. Remove from the oven, allow to cool in the pan for a few minutes and then gently turn them out onto a cooling rack.

If you do not have a donut pan, divide the batter among 6 greased wells of a muffin pan and bake at 350°F (176°C) for 20 to 23 minutes, or until a toothpick inserted into the middle of a muffin comes out clean. For donut holes, divide the batter among the wells of a mini muffin pan and bake at 350°F (176°C) for 8 to 10 minutes.

(continued)

coating

½ cup (110 g) vegan butter (optional)

½ cup (100 g) cane or granulated white sugar

2 tbsp (15 g) ground cinnamon

Coat the donuts. While the donuts are still a little warm, gently melt the vegan butter in a microwave or in a pan over a very low heat on the stovetop. In a bowl big enough to fit the donuts into for dipping, combine the sugar and cinnamon. Using the butter ensures a good amount of sugar sticks to the donuts and helps give a "fried" flavor. However, if you want to keep the recipe oil-free, you can omit the butter, dipping the donuts into the cinnamon-sugar mixture while they are hot, and it will stick to them quite well.

Take each donut and dip it into the butter on each side and all around the edges then immediately place in the cinnamon-sugar mixture and coat on all sides. Be really generous with the sugar coating.

They are best eaten freshly made but will keep for 2 to 3 days in a sealed container.

tip: The donuts (without the coating) can be frozen for up to 2 months. Thaw overnight in the refrigerator and warm for a few seconds in a microwave or for 5 minutes in a 375°F (190°C) oven; then coat as directed.

"I ONLY HAVE PIES FOR YOU" SWEET POTATO PIE

yield: 8 to 10 slices

1 (10" [25.5-cm]) Simple Pastry Pie Crust (page 195), prebaked

filling

1 (13.5-oz [400-ml]) can full-fat coconut milk (it must be full fat and not light)

2 very packed cups (266 g) baked and peeled sweet potato or yam (about 2 medium potatoes; must be the orange-fleshed variety, not white)

¾ cup (165 g) dark brown sugar

¼ cup (32 g) arrowroot powder or cornstarch

1 tbsp (15 ml) vanilla extract

½ tsp salt

1 tsp ground cinnamon

½ tsp ground nutmeg

⅛ tsp freshly ground black pepper

¼ tsp ground ginger

⅛ tsp ground cloves or allspice

Move over, pumpkins. As lovely as you are, sweet potatoes make a far tastier pie! Plus, they are available all year round, so you don't have to wait for fall to indulge. This delicious dessert has all sorts of good going on with the roasted sweet potato, creamy coconut milk and the copious amount of brown sugar and spices that go into making the custard. Don't get freaked out by the black pepper. It might sound strange, but it adds a certain something that no one will be able to put their finger on, and it's so good! The candied pecans, while not mandatory, are highly recommended for extra texture and flavor. They are amazing on their own as a snack, too!

Preheat the oven to 350°F (176°C) with a baking sheet in there to heat up. You will need it later. Have the prebaked crust ready.

Prepare the filling. In a blender, combine all the filling ingredients and blend until completely smooth and velvety. Pour into the pastry case, smooth out the top and place on the preheated sheet. Bake for 50 to 55 minutes. The filling should feel just set if you gently press in the center, with a little bit of wobble.

Remove from the oven and allow to cool completely before refrigerating for at least 1 hour before serving.

To prepare the pecans, in a small bowl, toss the nuts with the maple syrup, brown sugar and as much salt as you like; ½ teaspoon will give them a salty edge once baked and it works really well with the sweet pie. Use less salt if you prefer.

(continued)

"I ONLY HAVE PIES FOR YOU" SWEET POTATO PIE (CONTINUED)

candied pecans

1 cup (100 g) pecans

2 tbsp (30 ml) pure maple syrup

2 tbsp (28 g) dark brown sugar

¼ to ½ tsp salt

to serve

Vegan whipped cream

Spread out the nuts on a parchment paper–lined baking sheet and bake at 350°F (176°C) for 10 minutes. They will be bubbling and sizzling. Don't leave them in the oven for any longer as they will burn. Remove from the oven, allow to cool on the paper, and gently separate them. Once cool, store in a sealed container.

Serve the pie with vegan whipped cream and a tumble of candied pecans. For an extra-decadent twist, try serving the pie with the caramel sauce from my Saucy Salted Caramel Chocolate Brownies recipe (page 167). They work together beautifully!

Leftover pie, if wrapped well, will keep for up to a week in the fridge.

tip: Bake the sweet potatoes in their skins, and then scoop out the flesh. I do not recommend using canned sweet potato or steamed or boiled sweet potato to make this pie. The flavor and texture is much better because none of the lovely flavor gets diluted. Simply prick the sweet potatoes all over, 5 or 6 times with a fork, and place on a baking sheet in a preheated 400°F (200°C) oven. The baking time will vary, depending on their size, but it's usually somewhere between 40 and 60 minutes. Test them by poking them with a fork. Remove them from the oven when they are soft. You can do this up to 4 days in advance and store the cooked potatoes in the fridge.

SKY-HIGH APPLE PIE

yield: 10 to 12 servings

filling

4½ lb (2 kg) apples (about half and half Granny Smith and Golden Delicious or Braeburn)

2 tbsp (30 g) vegan butter

⅓ cup (70 g) light or dark brown sugar

½ tsp ground cinnamon

¼ tsp ground nutmeg

¼ tsp salt

2 tbsp (19 g) cornstarch or arrowroot powder

2 tbsp (30 ml) apple cider vinegar

crust

3½ cups (438 g) all-purpose flour, plus more for dusting

½ cup (56 g) almond flour or meal (or use more all-purpose flour, for nut-free)

¾ cup + 2 tbsp (200 g) vegan butter

⅓ cup (67 g) granulated white or cane sugar, plus more for sprinkling

¼ tsp salt

About ½ cup + 2 tbsp (150 ml) iced water

Even the word pie is comforting, homely and nostalgic, and it's hard to deny the temptation of golden-crusted pastry, wrapped around soft, sweet, juicy apples. I don't call this pie "Sky-High" lightly. It really is tall and perfectly domed, and it stays that way when baked because the apples are precooked before the pie is assembled. All the shrinking happens on the stove, so you aren't left with an empty, collapsing dome of pastry when the pie is baked. I like to use two varieties of apple for optimum filling texture, and a little vinegar helps balance the sweet flavor with a bit of tartness. When it comes to the pastry, nonvegan sweet pastries often have egg in them for extra richness. I like to use almond flour in mine to emulate that richness.

Prepare the filling. Peel, core and slice the apples into chunky wedges about ⅛ inch (3 mm) thick.

In a very large saucepan, melt the vegan butter over medium-low heat, and then add the sugar, cinnamon, nutmeg and salt. Once the sugar has melted into the butter, add the apple slices and stir to coat them all in the buttery liquid. Cook them for about 10 minutes, or until just beginning to soften.

Meanwhile, place the cornstarch in a small bowl. Stir in the vinegar until smooth, to create a slurry. Once the apples are done cooking, remove from the heat and stir in the cornstarch slurry; then allow to cool completely. If you need to hurry them up, you can spread them out in a thin layer on a large baking sheet or platter. The filling can be prepped up to 3 to 4 days in advance and stored in a sealed container in the fridge.

Prepare the crust. In a food processor, combine all the crust ingredients except the ice water. Pulse about 10 times, until the mixture looks like coarse bread crumbs, then add the water gradually and keep pulsing until the pastry starts to come together. Do not overmix; gently pulsing it is enough. With the machine turned off, lift the processor's lid and feel the dough to see whether it is moist enough to ball up. It should be just tacky but not wet. As soon as it is coming together, remove the blade and form the dough into a ball, handling it as little as you possibly can. Then, wrap it in plastic wrap and chill in the fridge for at least 45 minutes; up to 2 days is fine.

(continued)

"egg" wash

1 tbsp (15 ml) nondairy milk

1 tbsp (15 ml) pure maple syrup

1 tbsp (15 ml) melted vegan butter or oil

Preheat the oven to 375°F (190°C) with a baking sheet on the middle shelf and dust a clean work surface with a generous amount of flour. Take the pastry dough from the fridge, unwrap it and cut it in half. Rewrap one piece and put it back in the fridge until you have rolled the bottom crust; place the other half on the prepared work surface.

Have a 10-inch (25.5-cm) pie dish ready. Dust the top of the pastry with some more flour and roll into a circle a little bigger than the pie dish. Wrap the pastry dough around the rolling pin and carefully unroll it over the dish. Press it in gently all around so it's sitting snugly, and carefully spoon in the prepared apples. Pack the apples down tightly and heap them up in the middle into a dome shape.

Remove the remaining pastry dough from the fridge, dust with flour and roll into a circle big enough to cover the top of the pie dish. Wrap the pastry dough around the rolling pin and carefully unroll it over the top so it's sitting snugly over the apples. Press it down gently all around the edges, then trim off the excess with kitchen scissors or a sharp knife. Crimp by hand or use a fork to press little indentations all around the outside.

If you want to decorate the top, roll out any remaining pastry dough again and cut shapes, arranging them gently on the top of the pie.

Prepare the "egg" wash. In a small bowl, mix together the "egg" wash ingredients and brush them really generously over the top of the pie.

Finally, cut a 1-inch (2.5-cm) cross in the center of the crust to allow steam to escape, sprinkle the top all over with sugar and place the pie in the oven on the hot baking sheet. Bake for around 60 minutes, or until a lovely golden brown. Serve immediately.

Once cooled, the pie will keep, covered, for up to 5 days in the fridge. You can reheat the entire pie in a 350°F (176°C) oven for 30 minutes, or individual slices for 1 to 2 minutes in a microwave.

tip: The unbaked pie can be frozen and baked later, but I would recommend using a metal pie dish if doing this, as a ceramic or glass dish could shatter when going straight from freezer to oven. Wrap the pie tightly in plastic wrap or aluminum foil before freezing, and when you want it, unwrap and bake straight from frozen for an extra 15 to 20 minutes.

THE GREAT BRITISH BAKEWELL TART

yield: 8 to 10 servings

1 (10" [25.5-cm]) Simple Pastry Pie Crust (page 195), prebaked

1⅔ cups (208 g) all-purpose flour

½ cup + 2 tbsp (70 g) almond flour

⅔ cup (133 g) white granulated or cane sugar

1¼ tsp (5 g) baking powder

Slightly heaping ¼ tsp baking soda

¼ tsp salt

1 cup (240 ml) unsweetened nondairy milk

2½ tsp (13 ml) apple cider vinegar (see note on page 38)

1½ tsp (8 ml) almond extract

⅓ cup (80 ml) melted vegan butter or coconut oil

1 cup (320 g) room-temperature raspberry jam

A true British classic, this tart is thought to originate from the town of Bakewell in Derbyshire. It's a really popular teatime treat and one that my mum made a lot when I was growing up. I just had to veganize it! There are so many comforting elements to this tart. First, there is a crispy, pastry crust covered in a generous smear of raspberry jam, and then there is a thick layer of almond-y sponge. Purists stop there, except for maybe a scattering of almonds, but I like to add a blanket of smooth, brilliant white frosting and a scattering of almonds. It makes it look pretty, and if you are going to dessert, you might as well do it extravagantly!

Preheat the oven to 350°F (176°C) with an empty baking sheet on the middle shelf. Have ready the prebaked crust.

In a medium bowl, whisk together the all-purpose flour, almond flour, sugar, baking powder, baking soda and salt.

In another bowl, mix together the nondairy milk, vinegar, almond extract and melted vegan butter.

Spread the jam evenly in the bottom of the pastry case. If your jam is a little stiff, you can loosen it up before you start by warming it in a microwave for 5 to 10 seconds.

Next, pour the wet ingredients into the dry and fold them together gently. It is important not to overmix. Just do it enough to incorporate all the dry flour and work out any big lumps.

Spoon the cake batter over the jam in the pastry case. Don't just dump it all in the center, as it will make the jam move out to the edges. Spoon it on in blobs so it covers most of the surface, and then use a spatula to spread it out so it reaches the sides. Try to push it right up to the pastry so that it creates a seal and prevents the jam from bubbling through as it cooks, but don't worry if a few little streaks of jam make it up through the batter.

Place the tart on the hot baking sheet and bake for 40 minutes, or until a toothpick inserted into the middle of the cake comes out clean. Remove from the oven and let cool in the pan on a cooling rack.

(continued)

1 handful toasted flaked almonds, for decoration

1 cup (130 g) powdered sugar

1½ to 2 tbsp (22 to 30 ml) water

If your flaked almonds aren't of the already toasted variety, now is the time to do it. Heat a dry skillet over medium heat and add the almonds. Let them toast gently for a few minutes, until golden; then flip them over and toast the other side. Gently tip them out onto a plate to cool.

Once the tart is completely cool, place the powdered sugar in a bowl and mix in the water very gradually, 1 teaspoon at a time. It won't look like it will be enough, but once you get stirring, it will be. You need the icing to have a thick, dropping consistency. Stop adding water once it gets to that stage and place your toasted almonds ready beside you.

Pour or spoon the icing over the top of the cake, starting in the center and allowing it to spread itself out, giving it a hand with a wet spatula if it all starts running in one direction and also to cover any gaps. The pastry crust should prevent it from running off, but a few drizzles look nice if it gets up and over. Immediately top evenly with the toasted almonds before the icing has a chance to set. It doesn't take long, so be quick.

tip: Raspberry jam is my favorite for this recipe because of its slight tartness, but strawberry or cherry also works really well.

LUSCIOUS LEMON DRIZZLE CAKE

yield: 12 slices

cake

⅓ cup (67 g) soft room-temperature vegan butter, plus more for pan

1½ cups (300 g) cane or granulated white sugar, plus more for pan

¾ cup (180 ml) aquafaba (typically the amount you get from a 19-oz [540-ml] can—see note on page 18)

Zest of 2 lemons

6 tbsp (90 ml) fresh lemon juice

½ cup (123 g) unsweetened applesauce

1 tsp salt

1 tsp vanilla extract

⅓ cup (80 ml) unsweetened nondairy milk

3 cups (375 g) all-purpose flour

2 tbsp (22 g) baking powder

Sharp with bright lemon flavor and rich with vegan butter and sugar, this cake is a real treat. Even in the dreary depths of winter, it will make you feel as though it's spring. This cake can "wear" its frosting in two ways: You can go down the classic drizzle route and pour it over the cake while it is still warm, making it really sticky and moist; or you can wait for the cake to cool, and then pour it on, so it ends up with thick, smooth, soft frosting like my version in the picture. If you use the latter method and feel like getting fancy, I totally recommend adding some fresh or dried lemon slices or zest and some edible flowers to the top. They look so pretty against that smooth, brilliant white background. Just perfect for a lemon-loaded celebration cake!

Preheat the oven to 350°F (180°C) and grease an 8- or 9-inch (20.5- or 23-cm) round cake pan that is at least 3 inches (7.5 cm) deep. Line the bottom with a circle of parchment paper, and sprinkle a little sugar all around the edges of the cake pan. Tip out any excess that does not stick to the buttery sides of the pan.

In a large bowl or a stand mixer, beat together the sugar and vegan butter really well for 3 to 4 minutes.

In another bowl, combine the aquafaba, lemon zest and juice, applesauce, salt, vanilla and nondairy milk, and whisk them together well.

Sieve the flour and baking powder into the butter mixture. Stir together gently by hand or on the lowest mixer speed, and then gradually pour in the milk mixture, a few tablespoons at a time, mixing gently as you go, until a thick batter is formed. Do not overmix. Be gentle and keep going only until all the dry flour has been combined. A few small lumps are fine.

Spoon into the prepared cake pan and bake in the middle of the oven for 45 to 50 minutes. The cake should be coming away from the edges of the pan, and if you press gently in the middle with a finger, it should spring slowly back. A toothpick inserted right into the middle of the cake should come out clean. Turn out, very gently, onto a cooling rack and peel off the parchment paper. If it is a little stuck around the edges because the sugar has baked on, just gently run a knife around the edges first.

(continued)

LUSCIOUS LEMON DRIZZLE CAKE (CONTINUED)

icing

1¾ cups (210 g) powdered sugar

About ¼ cup (60 ml) fresh lemon juice

You can either ice the cake while it is still warm or wait until it is completely cool. If you ice while warm, first pierce some holes all over the top to help the icing seep into the sponge. You'll get a really sticky, moist, drizzle cake. If you allow the cake to cool before topping with icing, you do not need to pierce holes in it. The icing will set to a thicker, soft, smooth and less sticky consistency.

Prepare the icing. Place the powdered sugar in a bowl and gradually add the lemon juice, 1 tablespoon (15 ml) at a time, stirring well as you go. Although ¼ cup (60 ml) of juice should be about right, it will vary slightly every time. You might need a tiny bit more, but don't overdo it, as you want to keep it nice and thick. The texture needs to be thick and glossy, yet pourable and spreadable. If you accidentally add too much liquid, you can add a little more powdered sugar to thicken it up again. Ice the cake as directed, according to your preference.

tips: Turn this into a layer cake by cutting the sponge in two horizontally and filling with buttercream. You can use the buttercream recipe from my Jam-tastic Victoria Sponge Cake on page 139. Add 1 to 2 tablespoons (6 to 12 g) of grated lemon zest to it to give a lovely lemon flavor that will complement this cake.

The leftover drained chickpeas can be frozen until you need them, or you can use them to make my Feel-Good Potato and Chickpea Curry (page 101).

PEANUT BUTTER NUTTER CHOCOLATE CAKE

yield: 9 servings

cake

Oil or vegan butter, for pan

⅓ cup (86 g) natural peanut butter (see tips)

1½ cups (360 ml) unsweetened nondairy milk

2 tsp (10 ml) vanilla extract

½ cup (123 g) unsweetened applesauce or peeled and pureed cooked sweet potato

2 tbsp (30 ml) apple cider vinegar (see note on page 38)

½ tsp instant coffee or espresso powder (optional but recommended; it really brings out the chocolate flavor)

2 cups (250 g) all-purpose flour

1 cup (200 g) cane or granulated white sugar

¾ cup (65 g) unsweetened cocoa powder

2 tsp (8 g) baking soda

1 tsp baking powder

½ tsp salt (use only ¼ tsp if your peanut butter contains salt)

½ cup (90 g) vegan chocolate chips (see note on page 37)

Chocolate and peanut butter, together, should rule the world. They could solve all of life's problems, and that's why I'm bringing you this in-your-face, intensely chocolaty cake with drippy, sticky, sweet, peanut butter glaze. If you're feeling down, this is what you need. It's the ultimate comfort food cake. I'll be honest and say that I'm not usually the biggest fan of chocolate cake because it tends to be a bit dry and lacking in flavor. Fear not here, though, because this one is stick-to-the-fork moist and stays that way for days. This recipe has no added oil or vegan butter in the sponge. Peanut butter acts as the fat, adding to the rich flavor and the slightly fudgy texture.

Prepare the cake. Preheat the oven to 350°F (176°C) and grease an 8-inch (20.5-cm) square pan with oil or vegan butter. Cut a rectangle of parchment paper as wide as your pan and long enough to cover the bottom and 2 opposite sides with enough overhang to act as handles for lifting out the cake once it's been baked. The oil or butter will help keep it in place.

Put the peanut butter in a bowl and gradually add the nondairy milk, whisking as you go, to incorporate the peanut butter into the milk. Then add the vanilla, applesauce, vinegar and coffee; stir together really well.

In another bowl, whisk together the flour, sugar, cocoa powder, baking soda, baking powder and salt.

Pour the peanut butter mixture into the flour mixture and stir together gently. Do not beat it and do not overmix; stop when all the flour has just been absorbed. Add the chocolate chips and gently stir again to distribute. Then immediately pour into the prepared pan and bake for 37 to 40 minutes, or until the cake is coming away from the edges and, if you press on the top of it with a finger, it feels firm with a little bit of give. A toothpick inserted into the middle should come out almost clean. You might hit a melted chocolate chip, so bear that in mind when checking. To keep the cake nice and moist, it is important not to overbake it. It's better to underbake it very slightly.

(continued)

PEANUT BUTTER NUTTER CHOCOLATE CAKE (CONTINUED)

frosting

¾ cup (194 g) natural peanut butter

¼ tsp salt (use only ⅛ tsp if your peanut butter contains salt)

1 cup + 2 tbsp (146 g) powdered sugar

4 to 7 tbsp (60 to 105 ml) unsweetened nondairy milk

Remove the cake from the oven and lift it gently out of the pan, using the parchment paper "handles." Place on a cooling rack and allow to cool completely before frosting.

Prepare the frosting. In a medium bowl, beat the peanut butter with the salt until fluffy. Gradually add the powdered sugar, beating as you go. It will likely get a little stiff, and when it does, add nondairy milk a tablespoon (15 ml) at a time, stopping when it reaches a thick, gloopy, yet pourable consistency.

Place the cake on a plate, and then pour the frosting over the cake, using a spatula to spread it out, if necessary. It will run down the sides in places. Allow the frosting to firm up a little before serving. You can hurry it along by chilling it in the fridge for around 30 minutes.

tips: *Use either smooth or crunchy peanut butter. Smooth looks better but crunchy adds good texture!*

Mashed banana used instead of the applesauce or sweet potato is really nice!

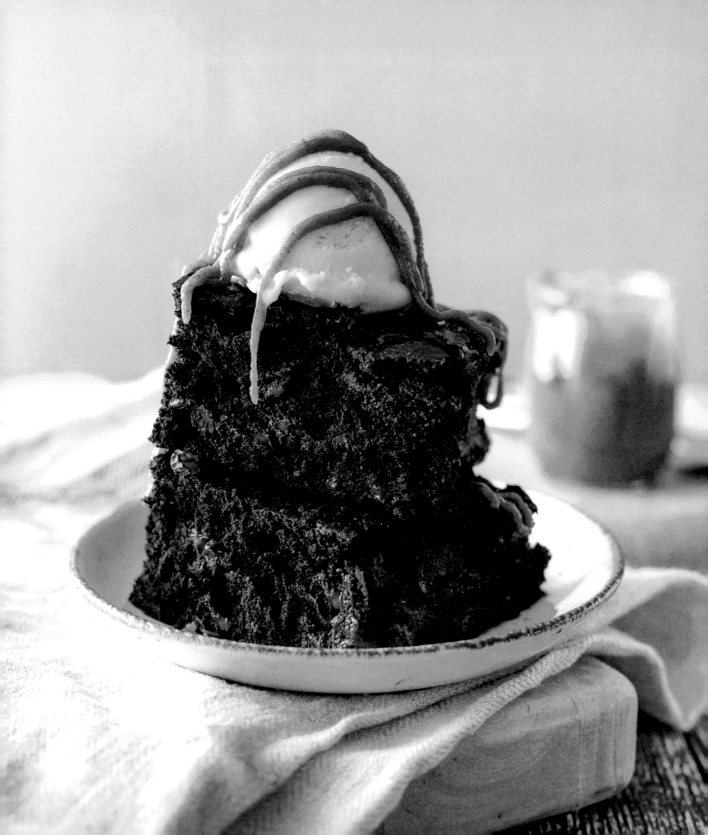

SAUCY SALTED CARAMEL CHOCOLATE BROWNIES

yield: 9 servings

brownies

Vegan butter or oil, for the pan

¼ cup + 2 tbsp (90 ml) aquafaba (see note on page 18), or 2 tbsp (14 g) ground flaxseeds plus 5 tbsp (75 ml) warm water

1 cup (86 g) unsweetened cocoa powder

½ packed cup (110 g) dark brown sugar or coconut sugar

½ cup + 1 tbsp (135 g) natural almond butter

⅓ cup (80 ml) pure maple syrup

2 tsp (10 ml) vanilla extract

½ tsp salt

1 tsp instant coffee or espresso powder

⅓ cup (80 ml) unsweetened nondairy milk

⅔ cup (84 g) all-purpose or whole wheat flour (for gluten-free, use ⅔ cup [67 g] oat flour or 1⅓ cups [129 g] almond flour)

1 tsp baking soda

1 tsp baking powder

1 cup (175 g) vegan chocolate chips (see note on page 37)

This recipe is for serious dessert lovers only. Buckle up and prepare to be blown away by these dense, fudgy, gooey and chocolaty squares with super-rich, sweet and seriously delicious caramel sauce. They will, for sure, change the way any skeptic feels about vegan desserts, and they will also more than likely change the way your pants fit unless you manage to exercise some self-control. I love to serve these brownies warm, topped with dairy-free vanilla ice cream and a very generous drizzle of the warm caramel sauce. The ice cream slowly melts over the gooey brownies and combines with the caramel to form rivers of sweetness that drizzle down and into the bottom of the bowl . . . (drool).

Preheat the oven to 325°F (162°C) and grease an 8-inch (20.5-cm) square pan with oil or vegan butter. Cut a rectangle of parchment paper as wide as your pan and long enough to cover the bottom and 2 opposite sides with enough overhang to act as handles for lifting out the cake once it's been baked. The oil or butter will help keep it in place.

If using ground flaxseeds instead of aquafaba, place in a cup or small bowl and mix with the warm water now and let thicken for 5 minutes.

In a food processor, combine all the brownie ingredients, except the chocolate chips, and process until smooth. Add the chocolate chips and pulse 2 or 3 times to distribute them evenly throughout the batter. Scoop the thick and gloopy batter into the prepared pan and level off the top. If you struggle, dip a spatula in a glass of water, and spread the batter with it. It will make it much easier. Bake for about 35 minutes, or until the outside feels springy and the inside is not liquid, but when a toothpick into the middle is inserted, it comes out a little sticky with chocolaty goo. Remove from the oven and allow to rest in the pan for at least 30 minutes before serving.

(continued)

SAUCY SALTED CARAMEL CHOCOLATE BROWNIES (CONTINUED)

caramel sauce

½ cup (110 g) dark brown sugar or coconut sugar

2 tbsp (30 ml) water, plus more as necessary

2 tbsp (30 g) almond butter

2 tbsp (30 g) vegan butter or coconut oil

⅛ tsp salt, or up to ¼ tsp, to taste

To prepare the caramel sauce, in a small saucepan, combine all the caramel ingredients and heat over a medium-low heat, stirring, until it just starts to bubble and becomes really melty, saucy and you can't see any sugar grains. It should take a maximum of about 7 minutes. If it is too thick, you can add a little more water to thin.

Remove the brownies from the pan, loosening the sides with a spatula or pallet knife, if necessary, and cut into either 9 large squares or 16 smaller squares. They are very rich when served with the sauce, so you don't need a huge portion, no matter what your eyes tell you!

Serve the brownies drizzled with warm caramel sauce.

tips: Warm leftover brownies in a microwave for 20 seconds to make them super soft and squidgy again.

Leftover caramel sauce can also be warmed for 10 to 15 seconds in a microwave or over low heat on the stovetop to return it to its saucy glory.

To make the recipe nut-free, use sunflower seed butter or tahini in place of the almond butter.

ULTRA DECADENT PEANUT BUTTER ICE-CREAM CAKE

yield: 6 servings

ice-cream cake

Vegan butter or coconut oil, for pan

18 (200 g) vegan chocolate sandwich cookies (see tip)

¼ cup (28 g) vegan butter or coconut oil, melted

1 cup (260 g) natural peanut butter

4 medium ripe and spotty bananas

¼ cup + 2 tbsp (75 g) coconut sugar or brown sugar

1 tsp vanilla extract

¼ tsp salt (omit if your peanut butter contains salt)

I like this recipe because it looks and tastes as if a lot of work went into it, when in fact, all that is involved is a little blending and stirring. You really can't go wrong when things start with a rich, buttery, chocolate cookie crust, a peanut butter and banana ice-cream topping and borderline-inappropriate peanut butter fudge sauce. And yes, we are making ice cream from scratch in minutes with no churning involved. How is that even possible?

This is a great dessert for making ahead or for having in the freezer as an emergency standby in case of company, and children love it. It's worth knowing that any nut or seed butter can be used instead of the peanut butter, making it a great option for children's parties.

Grease the bottom of a 6- or 8-inch (15- or 20.5-cm) springform pan with a tiny bit of vegan butter or coconut oil, and then line it with a circle of parchment paper. The butter or oil helps prevent the paper from moving around.

In a food processor, process the sandwich cookies until they have a fine crumb texture. Pour in the melted butter and process again until combined. Spoon into the bottom of the prepared pan and press down really hard all over, as evenly as you can, to compact it. Put it in the fridge or freezer while you make the filling.

In a food processor or high-powered blender, combine the peanut butter, bananas, coconut sugar, vanilla and salt. Blend until creamy and completely smooth.

Remove the pan from the fridge or freezer and evenly pour in the blended filling. Place in the freezer, making sure the pan is absolutely level, and leave for at least 4 hours, or until completely frozen.

(continued)

ULTRA DECADENT PEANUT BUTTER ICE-CREAM CAKE (CONTINUED)

peanut butter fudge sauce

1 cup (175 g) semisweet vegan chocolate chips or the same quantity from a bar (see note on page 37)

¼ cup (60 g) natural peanut butter

¼ cup (60 ml) canned light or full-fat coconut milk

1 tbsp (15 ml) pure maple syrup

Pinch of salt

to serve

Vegan cream of choice (optional)

Fresh banana slices (optional)

Roasted peanuts (optional)

Prepare the fudge sauce. In a saucepan, warm all the sauce ingredients over low heat, stirring occasionally, until it has all melted together.

Take the ice-cream cake out of the freezer at least 20 to 30 minutes before you want to serve it and remove it from the pan. To make it easier to release the pan, soak a dish towel in hot water from the tap, wring it out and fold it into a long, thin strip about as tall as the pan. Wrap it around the outside for 1 to 2 minutes. It will warm it just enough to release the cake from the edges. Then you can remove the sides of the pan, pull off the bottom, peel off the paper and place the cake on a serving plate.

Just before serving, top with your vegan cream of choice, banana slices and roasted peanuts, if desired. Once sliced and just as you are serving, pour a generous drizzle of warm fudge sauce over the cake. Alternatively, you can drizzle room-temperature sauce over the top as soon as you take the cake out of the pan so that it sets on contact with the freezing ice cream and makes a kind of fudgy magic shell.

Leftover fudge sauce can be stored in the fridge for up to a week and can be reheated gently in a pan or a microwave. Add more coconut milk to thin as needed.

tip: *For a healthier, gluten-free crust, substitute 2 cups (300 g) of raw cashews and 1½ cups (114 g) of unsweetened shredded coconut for the chocolate sandwich cookies.*

BAKED CREAMY COCONUT RICE PUDDING

yield: 6 servings

1 (13.5-oz [400-ml]) can full-fat or light coconut milk

4 cups + 3 tbsp (1 L) unsweetened nondairy milk (a coconut-derived one gives the best flavor)

2 tbsp (30 g) vegan butter (optional, but recommended for richness)

¾ cup (140 g) short-grain rice (such as Arborio or pudding rice)

½ cup (38 g) unsweetened shredded coconut, plus more for sprinkling

⅓ cup (67 g) granulated white or cane sugar

¼ tsp salt

1 tsp vanilla extract

¼ to ½ tsp ground nutmeg

Rice pudding has got to be one of the most soothing, comforting puddings of all. You can make a pretty decent one in a pan on the stovetop, but baking it slowly, the old-fashioned English-style way, makes it even better. It produces a luxuriously creamy pudding that can't be beat. Short-grain rice is a must as it gives the creamiest result, and I like to use canned coconut milk, too, for even more richness. As always, texture is important to me, which is why I also add some shredded coconut and finish the pudding under the broiler for a few minutes to get patches of blistered, darkly caramelized skin. Serve as it is, or with fresh fruit, such as mango or raspberries, chopped nuts, pumpkin seeds or quite simply with a big blob of jam for sheer comfort food heaven!

Preheat the oven to 350°F (176°C).

In a large saucepan, combine the 2 kinds of milk and the vegan butter (if using) and heat over medium heat until hot. Remove from the heat just before the mixture starts to bubble and boil.

Place a large baking dish (with at least a 2-quart [2-L] capacity) on a baking sheet. Combine the rice, coconut, sugar, salt and vanilla in the dish and pour the hot milk mixture over all. Stir well, and then sprinkle the nutmeg evenly over the top along with a little more shredded coconut. Place the dish and its baking sheet (in case of any overflow) into the oven and bake uncovered for 90 minutes, or until beautifully soft, thick and creamy.

Remove from the oven and either serve immediately or broil until the top is covered in dark brown, spotty patches. Best eaten hot.

tip: *Leftovers reheat well in the microwave or over low heat in a pan on the stovetop. Dilute with a little more milk if necessary.*

ROCKIN' RHUBARB CRUMBLE

yield: 8 servings

crumble topping

1½ packed cups (188 g) all-purpose flour

½ cup (110 g) vegan butter

½ heaping cup (120 g) sugar (I like to use a coarser variety, such as turbinado, for texture)

¾ cup (100 g) raw almonds (skin on is okay)

½ tsp salt

¾ cup (60 g) rolled oats

filling

9 to 10 large rhubarb stalks (1 kg), cleaned and chopped into 1" (2.5-cm) chunks (10 cups chopped)

½ cup (100 g) cane or granulated white sugar

2 tsp (10 ml) vanilla extract

¼ cup (32 g) arrowroot powder or cornstarch

1 tsp ground cinnamon

1 tsp ground ginger

If you are looking for a good, simple, comforting dessert, you can't do much better than rhubarb crumble. It is one of my favorites and takes me right back to my childhood. The sweet, buttery, nubbly crumble balances the tart, crimson, freckled rhubarb perfectly and the added nuts and oats give great texture. It's a dessert made for sharing. (Or not!) Serve it warm with vanilla ice cream; thick, rich custard or whipped coconut cream.

Prepare the crumble topping. In a food processor, combine the flour, vegan butter, sugar, almonds and salt and pulse for 1 to 2 minutes, or until the mixture is like coarse bread crumbs. The almonds will stay a little bigger and that's fine, as they add to the texture.

Alternatively, place the flour in a bowl and cut the butter into it or use your fingertips to rub it in. Then add the sugar and salt. Chop the almonds into chunky pieces and add those, too.

Remove the blade and transfer into a bowl, if necessary, and stir in the oats; then refrigerate for at least 30 minutes.

Meanwhile, preheat the oven to 400°F (200°C).

Prepare the filling. Place the chopped rhubarb in a large bowl. Sprinkle with the sugar, vanilla, arrowroot powder, cinnamon and ginger. Stir to combine everything, and then transfer to a baking dish no smaller than 9 x 9 x 3 inches (23 x 23 x 7.5 cm). Flatten out the rhubarb pieces as best you can and spoon the crumble topping over them. Don't pack down the topping; leave it a little bumpy-looking on top.

Set the baking dish on a baking sheet, place in the oven and bake for 45 minutes, or until golden and bubbling around the edges. Remove from the oven and let rest for at least 10 minutes before serving.

tips: *Change things up a little by replacing some of the rhubarb with sliced apple or strawberries. Just be sure to keep the overall quantity the same.*

To make the crumble nut-free, simply omit the almonds from the crumble topping.

LEGENDARY CHOCOLATE CHIP COOKIES

yield: 10 cookies

1 tbsp (7 g) ground flaxseeds

3 tbsp (45 ml) warm water

½ cup (110 g) room-temperature vegan butter

⅓ cup + 2 tbsp + 1 tsp (102 g) light brown sugar

3 tbsp (36 g) granulated white sugar

1 tsp vanilla extract

½ tsp fine salt

¼ tsp ground cinnamon

1¼ cups (157 g) all-purpose flour

½ tsp baking soda

½ cup (90 g) vegan chocolate chips (see note on page 37)

tips: *If you prefer a crunchier cookie, use these measurements for the sugar instead of those above and bake for 15 to 16 minutes:*

⅓ cup (70 g) light brown sugar
⅓ cup (67 g) granulated white sugar

Try sprinkling a little sea salt on top of each cookie before baking or add some chopped rosemary or orange zest to the dough for a lovely flavor variation.

Let's be honest here. Is there anything better than a fresh batch of chocolate chip cookies? I think not. And I take my cookie game very seriously. These cookies are perfectly soft and chewy, loaded with gooey chocolate chips and absolutely delicious. And never fear if you prefer a crunchy cookie, because I have included instructions on how to adjust the brown-to-white-sugar ratio to make them crunchier if you want to.

Preheat the oven to 350°F (176°C) and line a cookie sheet with parchment paper.

In a small bowl, mix the ground flaxseeds with the water and set aside.

In a mixing bowl, beat the vegan butter with the brown and the white sugar for about 2 minutes, or until smooth and creamy.

Add the vanilla, salt, cinnamon and flax mixture. Then beat again for 1 minute to incorporate.

Add the flour and baking soda and mix gently, just enough that everything is combined. Don't overmix.

Pour in the chocolate chips and stir to distribute.

Roll the cookie dough into balls, using 2 tablespoons (30 g) per ball, and place about 2 inches (5 cm) apart on the prepared cookie sheet, pressing down each ball with the palm of your hand or the back of a fork to flatten it to about ½ inch (1.3 cm) high.

At this stage, you can push a few more chocolate chips into the top to make the cookies look prettier, if you wish. Then place the cookie sheet in the oven on the middle shelf.

Bake for 13 to 15 minutes, depending on how soft you like your chocolate chip cookies. They will look a little underdone and feel soft but will firm up as they cool. Remove from the oven and leave on the cookie sheet for a few minutes; then carefully transfer them to a cooling rack.

ZESTY LEMON CHEESECAKE SANDWICH COOKIES

yield: 14 sandwich cookies

cookies

¾ cup (60 g) rolled or quick oats

2 cups (230 g) spelt flour, plus more for dusting

⅓ cup (70 g) light brown or turbinado sugar

1 tsp salt

1 tsp baking powder

⅓ cup + 1 tbsp (80 g) coconut oil (in solid form)

5 to 8 tbsp (75 to 120 ml) unsweetened nondairy milk

lemon cream

⅓ cup (67 g) vegan butter

2 cups (260 g) powdered sugar

1½ tbsp (23 ml) fresh lemon juice

Finely grated zest of 1 lemon

There is nothing like a sandwich cookie for comfort food appeal. These taste like lemon cheesecake with their sweet and slightly tart lemon cream, sandwiched between crisp, toasty, almost nutty tasting cookies. Every time I make a batch of these, they disappear within minutes of my putting them in the cookie jar!

For the cookies, preheat the oven to 375°F (190°C) and line a cookie sheet with parchment paper or a silicone mat.

In a food processor, process the oats until they have a coarse flourlike consistency. It should only take 20 to 30 seconds. Add the spelt flour, sugar, salt and baking powder and pulse a few times to combine. Then add the coconut oil and pulse again until it is combined and the mixture looks like coarse sand.

Gradually add the nondairy milk, 1 tablespoon (15 ml) at a time, pulsing between each addition, until a smooth dough forms. It will start balling up and if you touch it, it should feel slightly tacky but not sticky.

Dust a clean work surface with spelt flour. Transfer the dough onto it and lightly sprinkle it with a little more flour. Roll out evenly until about ⅛ inch (3 mm) thick; then use a 2- to 3-inch (5- to 7.5-cm) cookie cutter to cut rounds. If you don't have a cookie cutter, the rim of a glass or jar will work instead.

Place each disk on the prepared cookie sheet. They don't spread, so you don't need to leave much room around them. Just make sure they aren't touching.

Bake for 14 to 16 minutes, or until just starting to turn golden brown on the edges and bottom. The cookies will still feel a bit soft in the middle if you push with a finger, but they firm up as they cool. Carefully transfer each cookie to a cooling rack and allow to cool before sandwiching them together.

While they are cooling, prepare the filling. In a bowl, using an electric mixer or by hand, beat together the vegan butter, powdered sugar, lemon juice and zest until creamy. The mixture will look as if there is way too much powdered sugar when you start, but it will all come together. Don't be tempted to add more liquid as then the cream won't hold up between the cookies.

Once the cookies are completely cool, add a dollop of lemon cream on one side and sandwich it together with another cookie. Repeat until all the sandwiches are filled. Store in an airtight container.

UPPER-CRUST BREAD AND BUTTER PUDDING

yield: 6 servings

½ cup (110 g) vegan butter

8 to 9 (⅜" [1-cm]-thick) slices good-quality vegan white bread that is a few days old

1 cup (240 ml) unsweetened nondairy milk

6 oz (170 g) silken or soft tofu

1 tbsp (15 ml) vanilla extract

½ cup (100 g) white granulated or cane sugar

⅛ tsp ground cinnamon

⅛ tsp ground nutmeg

¼ tsp salt

¼ cup (80 g) marmalade or apricot jam, divided

¾ cup (110 g) golden raisins or sultanas

This is such a delicious, classic, comfort food dessert that I just had to put my stamp on it. It's pretty frugal, too, and if you have stale bread, it's the perfect way to put it to good use. Once baked, it's custardy on the inside; studded with soft, plump golden raisins; and buttery, golden and crusty on the top. Tofu makes a brilliant substitute for the eggs that would usually be used, and in a totally untraditional way, I love to brush the top with marmalade to make it sticky, shiny and chewy! I like to eat this as it is, but you could top it with vegan cream, ice cream or custard, if you want to.

Grease an 8-inch (20.5-cm) baking dish with a little of the vegan butter.

Spread each slice of bread generously with vegan butter, and then cut in half to make triangles. Arrange the slices, butter side up, in the dish. Don't pack them down as it's nice to have corners sticking up out of the custard, for texture.

In a blender, combine the nondairy milk, tofu, vanilla, sugar, cinnamon, nutmeg, salt and 2 tablespoons (40 g) of the marmalade. Blend until completely smooth.

Sprinkle the raisins over the bread slices, and pour the "custard" over everything. Use a finger to poke any raisins that are right on top in a bit, so they don't burn while baking. Leave to rest for around 30 minutes so the custard can soak into the bread. Preheat the oven to 325°F (162°C) while you are waiting.

Bake for 20 to 25 minutes, or until the custard is just softly set. Remove from the oven, brush the top all over with the remaining marmalade and place under the broiler for a couple of minutes so it goes golden, toasty and sticky. Keep a very careful eye on it because the corners of the bread will burn very quickly. Remove from the broiler and serve immediately while hot.

tips: *For a decadent twist, try soaking the raisins in brandy or rum for a few hours before adding them.*

You can swap out the bread for my Feelin' Fruity Yeast Bread (page 33) or use any other vegan fruit bread, hot cross buns, panettone or even croissants. Just make sure whatever you use is a few days old, so it soaks up the custard nicely.

SIMPLY PERFECT SNICKERDOODLES

yield: 9 cookies

cinnamon-sugar

¼ cup (50 g) white granulated or cane sugar

1 tsp ground cinnamon

cookies

¼ cup (50 g) coconut oil, soft but not liquid, or 3½ tbsp (50 g) soft but not liquid coconut butter

3 tbsp (45 ml) aquafaba (liquid from a can of chickpeas; see note on page 18)

2 tbsp (30 ml) pure maple syrup

⅓ cup (67 g) white granulated or cane sugar

1 tsp vanilla extract

1¼ cups (156 g) all-purpose flour

¾ tsp cream of tartar

¼ slightly heaped tsp baking soda

¼ tsp ground cinnamon

If you are craving cookie comfort, look no further than these soft, pillowy snickerdoodles with their glistening cinnamon-sugar crust. They are a timeless classic, and they come together from start to finish in less than 25 minutes. You can make them with coconut oil or, if you prefer oil-free baking, you can use coconut butter. There really isn't much difference in how they turn out. Aquafaba is again my egg replacer of choice because it makes these cookies exceptionally soft and light!

In a small bowl, mix the sugar and cinnamon together, so it will be ready for coating the cookie dough.

Preheat the oven to 375°F (190°C) and line a large baking sheet with parchment paper.

In a bowl, whisk together the coconut oil, aquafaba, maple syrup, sugar and vanilla until creamy and smooth.

Sift in the flour and add the cream of tartar, baking soda and cinnamon. Stir together gently. It is important not to overmix or beat the batter. If the mixture is too soft to roll, chill it in the fridge for 30 minutes to firm up first.

Roll the dough into balls about the size of walnuts (I use an ice-cream scoop), then roll each ball in the cinnamon-sugar and place about 2½ inches (6.5 cm) apart on the prepared baking sheet. Squash each ball down with the palm of your hand or with a fork until they are a little over ½ inch (1.3 cm) thick.

Bake for 9 to 11 minutes. After 9 minutes they will be slightly underdone and a little cookie dough–like in the center. I prefer them like that, but if you want them a little firmer, bake them for another minute or two. When you remove them from the oven, they will be soft. Allow them to cool on the baking sheet for about 5 minutes; then carefully transfer them to a cooling rack.

Once cool, store in an airtight container.

tip: *If you prefer no coconut flavor in your snickerdoodles, be sure to use refined coconut oil and not virgin coconut oil.*

CRISPY CRUNCHY CARAMEL POPCORN

yield: 6 cups (about 220 g)

⅓ cup (60 g) popcorn kernels

½ cup (100 g) coconut sugar

2 tbsp (30 ml) nondairy milk

2 tbsp (27 g) coconut oil

¼ cup (65 g) crunchy or smooth peanut butter

¼ tsp salt

½ cup (90 g) vegan chocolate chips (see note on page 37), or the same quantity from a bar

tip: *To make this recipe nut-free, use sunflower seed butter or tahini in place of the peanut butter.*

Snuggling in front of a movie is something we all enjoy, and a great movie just wouldn't be the same without popcorn. In true "me" style, though, this is not your average movie theater popcorn. I have actually never really liked that popcorn because of the texture. It's kind of soft, like stale crackers. So, I had to create my own super-crispy, amped-up popcorn. It's sweet, it's slightly salty, it's caramel-y and there's even some chocolate drizzled all over for good measure. My trick for ultimate crispiness? Bake it!

Preheat the oven to 300°F (150°C).

Heat a large, lidded saucepan over medium heat; then add the popcorn kernels and cover tightly.

Give the pan a shake every few minutes so the kernels don't burn. Before long, they will start popping. Keep them moving every 30 seconds or so, and as soon as the popping stops, remove the pan from the heat. Keep the lid on for a few minutes, just in case a rogue kernel decides to pop.

In a small saucepan, combine the coconut sugar and nondairy milk and heat over medium heat, stirring every few minutes until bubbles start to appear and the sugar has dissolved, 3 to 4 minutes. Remove the pan from the heat and add the coconut oil, peanut butter and salt. Stir really well until everything is smooth and combined. You can pop it back over low heat to loosen up the peanut butter a bit if you are struggling to mix it in.

Take the lid off the popcorn pan and pour the caramel sauce over the popped corn. Stir really well to coat every piece.

Line a baking sheet with parchment paper and evenly spread the popcorn on it in a single layer. Bake for 15 to 20 minutes, until it's really crunchy. Watch the popcorn very carefully near the end, as it can start to burn a little if left too long.

Remove from the oven and allow to cool completely on the baking sheet.

Melt the chocolate chips really gently at a low setting in the microwave or in a heatproof bowl set over a pan of simmering water on the stovetop; then drizzle all over the popcorn with a spoon.

Place the baking sheet in the fridge or freezer until the chocolate hardens up. Then break the popcorn into chunky pieces with your hands and transfer to an airtight container.

bits & bobs

We are coming to the end, but before I go, I want to share some of my favorite homemade bits and bobs that don't really fit into the other categories, but that I think are useful for you to have in your comfort food repertoire. These are basic recipes that I make over and over again in my kitchen and although they don't really hold up on their own, they do have the power to make other recipes or meals so much better.

LIFE-CHANGING VEGAN BUTTER

yield: about 1½ cups (335 g)

½ cup (56 g) almond flour

½ cup + 2 tbsp (150 ml) unsweetened nondairy milk

2 tsp (5 g) nutritional yeast (see note on page 49)

1 tsp salt

1 tsp apple cider vinegar

¼ cup + 2 tbsp (90 ml) mild olive oil (not extra-virgin unless you are okay with its flavor coming through)

1 cup (240 ml) melted room-temperature refined coconut oil (it must be refined, not unrefined or virgin)

Scant ⅛ tsp ground turmeric

When I tell people that I make my own vegan butter, they look at me in wonder, but the truth is, it is incredibly quick and easy to make with only a few simple ingredients. The hardest part is waiting for it to set in the fridge. The result is an incredibly rich and smooth "butter" that tastes just like buttery spread from the grocery store. Enjoy it in true comfort-food style, spread thickly on fresh bread (page 197) or English muffins (page 45), or cook yourself up some delicious treats. It works perfectly in baking and frosting!

In a blender, combine all the ingredients and blend until completely smooth, light and airy. In a high-powered blender, it will take less than 1 minute. Don't let the blender get too warm while blending or the butter could split a bit. If your blender does run a little warm, blend in short bursts and give it a break for a minute or two in between. Pour the liquid "butter" into a container, cover and refrigerate for a few hours until set.

tips: *Make your own almond flour by blending or processing blanched almonds in a food processor or high-speed blender. Stop as soon as they reach a flour consistency, though—otherwise you will end up with almond butter. A cup (110 g) of slivered almonds yields about 1 cup (110 g) of almond flour.*

My butter freezes incredibly well, so you can make a big batch and stash lots away for another day. I like to freeze it in ice cube trays so that I can pop out a little bit as I need it.

CHEESY BRAZIL NUT "PARM"

yield: 2½ cups (300 g)

1 cup (135 g) raw Brazil nuts, or almonds

¾ cup (115 g) raw cashew nuts

½ cup (56 g) nutritional yeast (see note on page 49)

1 tsp salt

½ tsp garlic powder

3 long strips lemon zest

If you miss having something cheesy to sprinkle on your meals, then this is the solution. I have a batch of this "Parm" in a jar in the fridge at all times. It takes a couple of minutes to make and keeps for weeks and weeks. It has a really deep, savory, cheesy flavor; a lovely crumbly, nutty texture; and the addition of the lemon zest adds a bit of sharp tang. Be ready to sprinkle it on everything!

In a food processor, combine all the ingredients and pulse—it's important to pulse and not run on full power, as otherwise you could end up with nut butter!— until the mixture looks like coarse bread crumbs. Then spoon into an airtight container and store in the fridge. It will keep for a couple of months.

TASTIEST ONION GRAVY

yield: about 3 cups (720 ml)

1 tbsp (15 ml) olive oil or water

2 medium onions, chopped

1 tbsp (7 g) nutritional yeast (see note on page 49)

2 tbsp (30 ml) tamari or soy sauce (see note on page 62)

2 tbsp (16 g) all-purpose flour, cornstarch or arrowroot powder

2 cups (480 ml) flavorful stock (I like to use mushroom stock)

The main components of a meal may get all of the attention, but it's the gravy that brings it all together. This is an easy onion gravy that is really tasty and will go with just about anything. It's thick, velvety and lump-free and can be made up to four days in advance. It freezes well, too, for ultimate convenience. Just let it defrost, and then warm through in a saucepan on the stovetop or in a microwave. Then drizzle it on everything!

Heat the oil or water (for oil-free cooking) in a small saucepan over medium heat and sauté the onions for 15 to 20 minutes, or until a deep golden brown. If using water to sauté, add more throughout the cooking process to prevent sticking. The more golden the onions get, the better your gravy will taste.

Transfer to a blender, add all the other ingredients and blend until very smooth.

Return to the saucepan and stir over medium heat, letting it bubble gently until thick and piping hot. If it becomes a little too thick for your liking, add a little boiling water and stir well until you get the consistency you like.

tip: *For special occasions, replace ½ cup (120 ml) of the stock with white wine (or Madeira or Marsala; red wine tastes good but makes the color a bit pink) and throw in a sprig or two of fresh herbs, such as rosemary or thyme. Add the herbs once it has been blended and returned to the pan, and scoop them out prior to serving.*

SIMPLE PASTRY PIE CRUST

yield: 1 (10-inch [25.5-cm])

½ cup (120 ml) water

2 or 3 ice cubes

2 cups (250 g) all-purpose flour, plus more for dusting

½ tsp salt

½ cup + 1 tbsp (120 g) very cold vegan butter, or ½ cup (108 g) refined coconut oil

¼ cup (50 g) white granulated or cane sugar (optional; for a sweet crust)

This simple pastry crust is perfect for making all your favorite sweet and savory tarts and pies. You can make it by hand or in a food processor. I always choose the food processor route because I'm lazy and it's so easy. This recipe makes enough for one 10-inch (25.5-cm) single crust. If you are making a double-crusted pie, simply double the recipe. Once you've mastered it, you will be baking tarts and pies like a pro!

In a glass, combine the water and ice cubes. Set aside.

In a food processor, combine the flour and salt. Add the vegan butter and pulse (don't run the food processor on full speed) until the mixture looks like coarse bread crumbs. Alternatively, if you don't have a food processor, in a bowl, combine the flour and salt, add the butter and cut it in with a pastry cutter or the tips of your fingers until it looks like coarse bread crumbs.

If you are making a sweet tart or pie and want a sweet crust, add the sugar now and stir to incorporate. If you are making a savory pie or tart, you do not need to add any sugar.

Next, gradually add the ice water, 1 tablespoon (15 ml) at a time, pulsing in between each addition, or use the blade of a dinner knife to stir the dough if mixing by hand. You will likely need 6 to 7 tablespoons (90 to 105 ml) of water, but it does vary depending on your brand of flour and humidity. Once it looks like it's starting to come together, get your hand in (fully stop the machine and be careful of the blade if using a processor) and check to see whether you can squeeze it together. It should be soft but not sticky. If it is too dry, add another drop of water and pulse or stir again.

Remove the blade and tip out (or simply place, if mixing by hand) the pastry dough on a lightly floured surface. Shape into a ball, only handling it as much as necessary, flatten to a disk and wrap in plastic wrap. Refrigerate for at least 30 minutes before using. Up to 2 days is okay or see the tips to follow my instructions for freezing.

(continued)

When ready to use, roll out the dough on a lightly floured surface until it is big enough to fit over the pie dish with some extra to spare. Gently roll the pastry around the rolling pin, lift it and drape it over the pie dish really carefully. Help it settle in and push it gently all the way around into the sides and the bottom. If you accidentally make a hole, tear a little from the overhang and patch it up. Use a sharp knife to trim the pastry around the edges so it's level with the top of the dish. Chill in the fridge for 30 minutes. This step is important and will prevent it from shrinking when you bake it.

Use as directed in your recipe, or to blind bake it, preheat the oven to 400°F (200°C) with a baking sheet on the middle shelf. Remove the chilled pastry case from the fridge and cut a square of parchment paper a little bigger than the pan. Screw it up into a tight ball as if you are going to throw it in the trash. Then pull it out flat again. This will help it sit in the case more easily. Carefully place it on the pastry case and fill with baking beads, rice or dried beans, and then bake for 20 minutes on the preheated baking sheet. Remove the paper and the baking beads really carefully, use a fork to prick holes all over the bottom, return the pastry crust to the oven and bake for another 5 minutes. Allow to cool completely before using in any recipe that calls for a blind baked or prebaked crust.

tip: Once made, and before rolling, the pastry dough can be frozen. Wrap it in plastic wrap, and then seal in either a freezer bag or freezer container. Let it defrost in the fridge for at least 7 hours, and use as needed.

BASIC CRUSTY WHITE BREAD

yield: 1 loaf

4 cups (500 g) all-purpose flour, plus more as needed

1 tbsp (10 g) instant or fast-acting yeast

2 tsp (10 g) salt

1 tbsp (12 g) granulated white or cane sugar (optional; see tips)

3 tbsp (45 ml) olive oil or melted room-temperature butter (optional; see tips)

About 1⅓ cups (320 ml) lukewarm water (not hot)

Oil or nonstick spray

Bread. Just a few, very simple ingredients, mixed together, kneaded and left alone for magic to happen. It's not nearly as difficult to make as you might think. Everything about the process is satisfying, from the fruity, yeasty smell of the dough, the kneading, seeing it rise, smelling it bake and finally, cracking into the golden crust and slathering it in my Life-Changing Vegan Butter (page 188). I could not even contemplate writing a book about comfort food without including a crusty bread recipe because it's one of the simplest, most popular comfort foods there is and just so happens to be one of my absolute favorites, too. I bake and eat way too much bread!

In the bowl of a stand mixer or a large bowl, stir together the flour, yeast, salt and sugar.

Add the oil and water, and—with the dough hook in place—knead for around 8 minutes on medium-low speed, or about 15 minutes by hand. Three to 4 minutes into kneading, turn the mixer off and give the dough a poke with your finger. It should feel tacky but not overly sticky. If it's too sticky, add another couple tablespoons of flour and if it's dry, add a tablespoon or two (15 or 30 ml) of water. Be sure not to add too much extra flour as it will affect the texture of your finished loaf.

Once the dough is very smooth and elastic, grease another bowl with a drop of oil or some oil spray, or lift the dough out of the one you mixed it in and use that one. Put the dough into the greased bowl and turn it all around in the oil so its surface is covered. Cover with a damp, clean dish towel (just run it under the tap for a few seconds, and wring it out) and leave on the kitchen counter until doubled. The time this takes will vary, depending on how warm your kitchen is, but bear in mind that the longer it takes to rise, the more flavor there will be, so unless you are in a hurry, don't rush it by cranking up the heat or putting it somewhere very warm. Mine generally takes between 60 and 90 minutes to double, and my kitchen is usually between 62 and 64°F (17 and 18°C).

(continued)

Once the dough has doubled, scrape it gently onto a clean, lightly floured work surface. Be careful not to tear it as you do this. Shape into a loaf by using the heels of your hands to flatten it into a rectangle roughly the width of a 9 x 5–inch (23 x 12.5–cm) loaf pan. Fold up the bottom third and use the heel of your hand to push it down and seal it a bit. Then fold the top third down (like an envelope) and push it down to seal it again. Then, fold the dough in half again and pinch closed all the way along the seam. Gently turn under the ends if they look a little untidy. Lightly oil the pan and place the dough in the pan.

Rub a little oil over the surface of the dough to prevent it from sticking, and then cover again with the damp dish towel. Leave until the dough is nicely domed and about 1 inch (2.5 cm) above the sides of the pan. It won't take as long this time, probably 30 to 40 minutes. While waiting, preheat the oven to 400°F (200°C).

Place in the center of the oven and bake for 35 to 40 minutes. The bread should be nicely brown on top and coming away from the edges. Remove from the pan and place on a cooling rack. If you knock on the bottom of the loaf, it should sound hollow.

tips: *To make a light, fluffy whole wheat loaf, replace up to half of the all-purpose flour with whole wheat flour.*

The sugar and oil can both be omitted, but the bread will take a little longer to rise, it will be crustier, it won't turn as golden and it won't keep as long.

Make bread rolls instead of a loaf. Shape into 6 equal-size balls and place about 1 inch (2.5 cm) apart on a parchment-lined baking sheet. Bake for around 25 minutes and test for doneness as described for a loaf.

EASY GARLIC RANCH DRESSING

yield: 8 to 10 servings

¾ cup (115 g) raw cashews (soaked in boiling water for 15 minutes then drained if you do not have a high-powered blender)

2 medium cloves garlic

1 tsp prepared yellow mustard

1 tbsp (15 ml) white wine vinegar

½ tsp cane or granulated white sugar or pure maple syrup

½ tsp salt, plus more to taste

Pinch of freshly ground black pepper, plus more to taste

½ to 1 cup (120 to 240 ml) water

½ tsp dried parsley

½ tsp dried dill

1 tbsp (3 g) chopped fresh chives, or 1 tsp dried

The only ranch recipe you will ever need. It will make even the dullest lettuce leaf taste amazing! Once you've got this in your back pocket, you are set for life. Make it as thick or thin as you like, and then use it as a dip, as a drizzle on your favorite salads, in potato salads, with pizza or, best of all, with my Bangin' BBQ Cauliflower Wings (page 109) because the two combined are just perfection!

In a blender, combine the cashews, garlic, mustard, vinegar, sugar, salt, pepper and ½ cup (120 ml) of water. Blend until completely smooth. Check the consistency and adjust it to suit your needs. If you are using it as a dip, it's best to leave it quite thick. If you are using it as a dressing, it's best to make it a bit thinner for drizzling. Just add more or less water to get your preferred consistency.

Add the parsley, dill and chives and pulse a couple of times to distribute. Add more salt and pepper to taste; then transfer to a sealed container and refrigerate. It will thicken over time and can be thinned with a few drops of water before serving.

tip: Adjust the garlic to suit your taste. It can even be omitted completely if you aren't a garlic fan.

thank you

First of all, I'd like to say a big thank-you to Page Street Publishing for allowing my dream of writing a book to come true. What an adventure it has been and I will be forever grateful.

Thank you to my family for their ongoing support and for putting up with me over the last few months. I won't lie; creating the recipes and writing this book has been an awful lot of work and things have gotten a little stressful at times. There have been tears, tantrums, overflowing sinks of washing up, canceled plans and some very random dinners, but we have come out the other side without too many complaints and are stronger for it.

A big, heartfelt thank-you to my team of amazing recipe testers, their families and their friends who loaned us their taste buds, too: Aoife Duggan, Colleen Neymeyer, Sharon Thomas, Sue Williams, Jessica Carlson, Carmen Muscalu, Victoria Parker, Lynne Wright, Patty Teruya, Rebecca L'Heureux, Judy Knutson, Jennifer Caruso, Julie Graham, Kerrin McLaughlin and Christine Smith. You stuck around throughout the whole process and have continued to support me even after testing was complete. I can never thank you enough for the time and effort you put into testing my recipes and the valuable feedback you provided. I suffer terribly from "imposter syndrome" and you have made me feel confident in putting this book and its recipes out into the wild.

Thank you to Chester for always being there to clear up the crumbs and debris from the kitchen floor and for providing snuggles and distraction when I was losing my marbles.

And last but definitely not least, thank you to my amazing readers: I am so grateful to you for your continued support and enthusiasm toward my recipes. Thank you for seeing something in me that I don't always see in myself. I value every single one of you as well as every single comment, photo, email and piece of feedback I receive. Know that I will forever be grateful to you for helping me find my life's purpose. I hope we get to continue on this adventure for a very long time to come!

Much love,

Mel x

about the author

Melanie McDonald is the creator of the popular food blog A Virtual Vegan, which has been showcasing her creative vegan recipes and photography since 2015. Her blog started as a hobby but the response to her writing and recipes was so positive that she soon found herself with millions of readers and ended up leaving her regular job to work full-time as a blogger, recipe creator, food writer and photographer. She is a regular contributing writer for Parade.com and her work has been featured by such media outlets as *Vegan Food & Living*, the BBC, *Huffington Post, Country Living, Reader's Digest, Better Homes & Gardens*, BuzzFeed, *Good Housekeeping, Cosmopolitan*, Food Network, MSN and many more.

Melanie grew up in the southwest of England and now lives on Vancouver Island in British Columbia with her husband, Paul; son, Jacob; and crazy dog, Chester. Her blog can be found online at www.avirtualvegan.com.

index